Thomas Day, John Adams

Reflexions upon the Present State of England and the

Independence of America

Thomas Day, John Adams

Reflexions upon the Present State of England and the Independence of America

ISBN/EAN: 9783337226473

Printed in Europe, USA, Canada, Australia, Japan

Cover: Foto ©Suzi / pixelio.de

More available books at **www.hansebooks.com**

REFLEXIONS

UPON THE

PRESENT STATE OF ENGLAND,

AND THE

INDEPENDENCE of AMERICA.

By THOMAS DAY, Esq;

Vedranfi fanguinofi battaglie; inauditi affedii; fpaventevoli facchi, in=
cendii, e rovini; fucceffi maritimi, che d'atrocitá non cederanno á
terreftri; e non meno atrocemente poi trafportate l'armi da vicini mari
d'Europa ne' piu remoti dell' Indie. Ufcirà frà l'armi qualche volta
ancora il negolio; e frá l'infano ftrepito della guerra, il defiderio natural
della pace Contuttocio prevaleranno poi fempre le rovine, le morti, e
le ftragi per ogni Cato. *Bentivoglio della guerra di fiandra.*

Our late delufions have much exceeded any thing known in hiftory, not
even excepting thofe of the crufades. For, I fuppofe, there is no ma-
thematical, ftill lefs an arithmetical demonftration, that the road to the
Holy Land, was not the road to Paradife, as there is, that the endlefs
encreafe of national debts is the direct road to national ruin.——So
egregious indeed has been our folly, that we have even loft all title to
compaffion, in the numberlefs calamities that are waiting us.
Hume's Hiftory of England : Vol. 5. P. 475.

LONDON:

Printed for J. STOCKDALE, oppofite Burlington-Houfe,
Piccadilly, 1782.

ADVERTISEMENT.

THE beginning of this eſſay was publiſhed
ſome weeks paſt in the London Courant.
Reaſons of a private nature prevented its continuance at that time; but the importance of the ſubject, and the critical ſituation of this country, induced the author to finiſh it and offer it to the
public in the form of a pamphlet. The haſte
with which it was written, and the neceſſity
of its immediate publication, may perhaps prove
ſome apology for any defects that may be found
in the ſtyle, method, or arrangement.

E S S A Y, &c.

ENGLAND is now placed in the moſt critical ſituation ſhe has ever experienced, ſince ſhe has poſſeſſed that degree of power and pre-eminence which ſhe has held for near a century, amongſt the neighbouring nations. Advanced by a variety of cauſes to that dangerous ſuperiority, which never fails to excite the jealouſy of every other people, that is placed within the ſphere of its attraction, ſhe has not been ſufficiently attentive to prevent by her moderation, that degree of envy which never fails to attend on greatneſs. Added to this, ſhe has miſtaken the very intereſts of her own ambition; and, inſtead of maintaining in perfect vigour thoſe reſources which would have overawed the jealouſy ſhe excited, ſhe has fooliſhly laviſhed them in the moſt wild, unprofitable manner, that ever diſgraced a nation. The Colonies, whoſe importance we now too late acknowledge,

B   appear

appear to have been the immediate caufes of her greatnefs. A country, prolific in all the articles either of neceffity or luxury ; a climate, varying through every degree of heat and cold ; an immenfe ocean, every where furnifhed with ports, and inviting the inhabitants to induftry and commerce : together with that extent of fertile foil, which feemed to allow the human fpecies liberty to expand for ages yet to come, were fuch advantages as no period of recorded time has ever feen attached to any other people in the univerfe. When we add to this, an identity of manners, language, prejudices, religion, nay, of intereft itfelf, it muft be confeffed that we have no reafon to expect a fimilar phænomenon, unlefs Providence, by the agency of its moft powerful inftruments of deftruction, fhould confound the pride of man, and lay the world which we inhabit wafte, that the human fpecies might begin their courfe anew.

But what Nature, which has fo widely feparated the two countries, had failed to do, what the united force of all the powers of Europe could not have effected, the wild ambition of one part of this nation, affifted by the vanity, blindnefs, and fupinenefs of the reft, has now perpetrated : America is now divided from the Parent Country, and leaves us nothing but the melancholy confolation of reflecting at leifure on what we have loft ; or forming fchemes which may at beft be vifionary,

vifionary, and fhould we fail in wifely managing, the laft ftake may be fatal.

I will not confume time to enumerate the complicated bleffings we have loft, or to execrate the felfifh and deteftable policy, which grafping at a toy, has thrown away the nobleft empire in the univerfe. I will confine myfelf to a fingle point, in the immenfe chaos of matter which rifes before me, and endeavour plainly and diftinctly to ftate the facts which are moft neceffary to be underftood and reafoned from, in our prefent fituation.

England is confeffedly in the moft critical fituation fhe has ever experienced; with ruined refources, her commerce almoft annihilated, her beft blood lavifhed on the deteftable fchemes of private ambition; her colonies exafperated by perfecutions and cruelties, too fhocking to be enumerated, and actually emancipated by fuccefsful refiftance from her dominion; her agriculture, the prop of every fociety, impaired, and her debts increafed almoft beyond the poffibility of further endurance; fhe ftands fingly forth upon the great theatre of the world, unfupported, unaffifted, to contend with three powerful nations, almoft as much for exiftence as for command and glory. The reft of Europe keeps aloof, attentive to the mighty conteft, and watching every opportunity to promote its refpective interefts, by the common mifchiefs of the combatants; nor is this

all,

all, every nation has in turn frowned upon the British advances, and shewed itself inimical to the cause in which we are engaged; nor can I entertain a single doubt, that had it been necessary to the purposes of the American independence, every other people would have succeffively come forward, and contended with us for the prize. Nature, or Providence, which directs the paffions of nations, like those of individuals, to the advancement of their own interefts, has, in this cafe, propofed two of the moft alluring objects which can act upon human avarice, or ambition; the abafement of an haughty rival, and the hopes of that immenfe fpoil which the emancipation of America prepares for Europe at large. Thefe difpofitions of our neighbours muft have been evident, from the very firft, to every man who caft the moft fuperficial view upon the ftate of things, or had the flighteft acquaintance with hiftory. The rulers of this country alone appear to have been unacquainted with thofe truths, which were revealed even to babes and fucklings; they feem to have imagined that France and Spain had forgotten their ancient hatred, their recent wounds; that Holland was become inattentive to her own commercial interefts; that every other nation would only fee things through the medium of the Britifh Miniftry; that every human paffion muft be hufhed, every human intereft fufpended,

while

while they were permitted to direct the tempefts they had raifed to the objects of their caprice or hatred. I need not here obferve how grofly, how fatally they have been difappointed; the final emancipation of America, the degradation of our naval honour, the lofs of almoft all our European and Weftern poffeffions, is the moderate price which this nation has already paid, for the implicit confidence which the Sovereign has repofed in his faithful and experienced fervants. Let us now enquire what are the meafures moft likely to procure our fafety, amidft thefe complicated diftreffes.

The original caufe of difpute between England and her Colonies, arofe from the claim of the Britifh Parliament to levy taxes upon the Americans, exerted in a trifling duty upon tea, impofed in the year 1767. But when, after the violence of the people of Bofton, committed upon the teas of the Eaft-India Company in 1773, feveral acts had paffed the Britifh Parliament, each encreafing in feverity, which annulled their government, abolifhed their houfes of affembly, deprived them of trial by jury, refigned their lives and property for every, and for no offence, into the hands of Governors nominated by the Crown; and, laft of all, abfolutely prohibited all commerce between the two nations, and permitted every act of hoftility to be exercifed upon

them :

them: the original caufe of oppofition was fwal-
lowed up in the immediate neceffity of yielding
to unconditional fubmiffion, or of boldly re-
pelling force by force. In confequence, therefore, of thefe precipitate and violent acts of the
Englifh Legiflature, which feemed to have no
other end than the extirpation of all liberty in
America, joined with the mighty preparations
made in this country to enforce them, the American Congrefs made a bold appeal to the firft
principles of human fociety, declared themfelves
independent of a country, which had deftined
them to flavery and deftruction, and invited the
reft of Europe to their alliance and affiftance.
It is evident, that from this moment the original
grounds of the quarrel were changed, and the
Americans no longer fought to refift, as fubjects,
the claim of taxation in the Britifh Parliament,
but to defend themfelves as independent nations,
from the attacks of an hoftile people, that exerted
all its force to reduce them to unconditional fervitude. On the contrary, the avowed end and
object of the war on the fide of England was
the reduction of fo many independent States to
its own dominion. The war which was afterwards begun with France has confeffedly the
fame object; fince it was not in confequence of
any national difpute with the country, but becaufe it fupported the freedom and independence

of

of the American States, that England thought it neceſſary to begin hoſtilities; and the treaty of alliance,
which was ſigned between the French Government and the Congreſs, on the 6th of January,
1778, expreſsly ſtates in the ſecond article, that,
" The eſſential and direct end of the preſent de-
" fenſive alliance is, to maintain effectually the
" liberty, ſovereignty, and independence, abſo-
" lute and unlimited, of the ſaid United States,
" as well in matters of government as of com-
" merce."

Hence it is plain, that the war which Great-
Britain has carried on with the Americans was at
the beginning, and has been at every inſtant of its
duration, till the laſt vote of the Houſe of Commons, ſtrictly ſpeaking, an offenſive war; that
this offenſive war has, in its conſequences, em-
broiled us with France, Spain, and Holland, and
ſtill ſubſiſts at this moment; ſince, however re-
ſpectable may be the opinion of ſo uncorrupt an
Houſe, it will not, I imagine, be pretended, that
it bears the authority of a law, in any other caſe,
than that of *diſqualifying* the people from chuſing
their own *repreſentatives.*

After having given theſe explanations, in order
to produce more clearly my ideas upon the ſubject, I ſhall reduce the queſtion to a ſingle alternative : Has Great-Britain abſolutely reſigned her
late ambitious views of conqueſt, or is ſhe ſtill
determined

determined to profecute the war, till it finally
terminate in either her own deftruction, or in
that of the American States? In the firft cafe, it
will be a confideration well deferving the attention
not only of the Government, but of the people at
large, by what means fhe may, with the greateft
celerity and honour, extricate herfelf from the
fatal labyrinth in which fhe is involved; in the
fecond, it will *only* be neceffary to add thirty millions more to the fupplies already voted, to raife
fixty or an hundred thoufand additional troops; in
order, not only to replace thofe we have loft by
ficknefs, by captivity, by combats, and by defer-
tion, but to enable our Generals to act offen-
fively, with better omens than they have hitherto
done. Should we take fuch vigorous meafures as
thefe, notwithftanding the immenfe difference of
the conteft, where the overflowing of our goals,
the ftarving remnants of our manufacturers, and
wretched German peafants, reluctantly contend
with the beft difciplined and moft warlike troops,
affifted, as often as neceffary, by the moft numerous militia in the world, and this in their
own country, where every thing is equally ad-
vantageous to them, and hoftile to us. Notwithftanding thefe immenfe difadvantages, I fhould
think we might fairly hope, by the end of another
campaign, for this is already loft, to be in poffeffion of another poft; at leaft, if we add to the

fpirited

xertions I have already n..
..eet of forty fail of the line, to preven.
French from pouring in their forces, and turnin
the balance in a critical moment.

But if thefe ideas are now reputed chimeric
and the experiment of a farther offenfive war i
rejected with abhorrence, not only by all d
cerning minds, but by our prefent Government,
fupported by a large majority of the people, I
apprehend it will-be neceffary to enquire, what
will prove the moft effectual and fpeedy means
of producing that peace, which is now become fo
neceffary to our fituation.

Thofe that have done me the honour to read
this crude effay with attention, will here, I imagine, anticipate the obvious anfwer which pre-
fents itfelf. For if the original and continued
caufe of war, has been the attempt of Great-
Britain to fubjugate the Independent States of
America to her dominion; if farther, Great-
Britain, contented with the loffes fhe has fuftain-
ed, finds herfelf in no condition to profecute the
claim, and is refolved to defift from an offenfive
war in America, it will neceffarily follow, that the
firft thing to be done is folemnly to defift from the
claim; and in defifting, to acknowledge the independence of America. By this one act, England
removes every caufe of animofity from between

C   her-

herfelf and the American States; by this one act fhe places herfelf upon the broad foundation of equity and reafon; frees herfelf from the neceffity of garrifoning pofts and cities which fhe cannot hold, is more collected for the defence of herfelf and her own undoubted rights, and ceafes to appear to the reft of Europe in the formidable light of an infolent, unjuft, and rapacious conqueror.

It may be here obferved, that fhould we take thefe fteps, fhould we even abandon New-York and Charles Town, which I fhould certainly think expedient to be done, the Americans are fo involved by the 8th article of the Treaty of Alliance, that they can make no feparate peace without the permiffion of the French.—I anfwer, that I think all ideas of peace, which are not equitable and general, and which do not extend to all the nations with whom we are at variance, are more calculated to pleafe a party, or ferve a Minifter, than to extricate the Englifh people from their prefent complicated diftreffes.

Since the beginning of the prefent fatal conteft, placed as I am at a diftance from the little interefts and paltry ambition, which dazzle fo many eyes, and turn them afide from the real purfuit of their country's welfare, I have remarked with wonder, the grofs falfities and impoftures which have fo often been current in this metropolis; and I muft own, that I have fometimes been

led

led to fufpect, that Heaven, in bereaving this
country of her former glory, was kindly preparing
its inhabitants for the ftroke, by depriving them
of their fenfes. For to what caufes, fhort of infatuation, can we attribute the various opinions
which have prevailed at different periods of this
difaftrous conteft; that the Americans would never
look the Britifh foldiery in the face; that a few
regiments would compleat the reduction of that
immenfe continent; that a majority of the Americans were attached to the Britifh government;
that the exchanging Philadelphia for Charleftown
was the fubjugation of America; that Lord
Cornwallis with an army of about ten thoufand
men, could penetrate and fubdue all the Southern
provinces; that the French would never affift the
Americans; and that all the nations of Europe
would tamely fuffer our maritime tyranny, and
the piracies of our privateers? To thefe might be
added, were it neceffary to fwell the catalogue,
many fentiments and obfervations of Lords and
great men of diftinguifhed abilities and importance; fuch as the opinion of a great Law-lord, that
the war in America was a defenfive war; the humane declaration of a late American Secretary,
that the Americans fhould be decimated with
more than Roman feverity; and his affertion, that
though the Americans had neither money or
credit, the Englifh government could raife troops

C 2   amongft

amongft them cheaper than the Congrefs: to thefe
might be added, the obfervation of a noble Lord,
about fix weeks before the furrender at York-town,
who, fpeaking of the Americans, faid, with an air
of triumph, " *Ils font au defefpoir*; and we are
juft going to eftablifh the civil government;" of
another, who after that furrender affirmed, " that
none but Britifh fools would be frightened at the
lofs of a few thoufand troops ;" and the opinion of
the greateft financier this country has ever feen
" that it was neceffary to maintain pofts in America, for the fake of *commerce*."

However extravagant thefe opinions and affertions, when thus crowded together, muft appear,
I believe there is no man moderately verfed in the
politics of this nation, during the laft ten years,
who has not feen them adopted as the principles of
our public conduct, or avowed by fome of the
moft diftinguifhed characters in the nation, as neceffary to be adopted ; nor fhould I repeat them,
in the midft of fo important a difquifition, if I did
not dread that fome new delufion might arife, deprive us of all our prefent hopes, and plunge us in
deeper mifery than we have yet experienced. The
prejudice which, I muft confefs, I more particularly dread at prefent is, that the Americans may
be induced to accept of peace, without our acknowledging their independence, and without our
comprehending their allies. Whence this opinion

should originate, unless from the selfish designs of
some men to consult their own avarice or ambition,
at the hazard of plunging this country a-new into
all the horrors of an inveterate civil war, and from
the general inattention of this people to procure
genuine information, I own I cannot compre-
hend. But to those who have only embraced these
da   opinions, because they are not used to
         themselves, I would propose the fol-
low   onsiderations: Did not the Americans,
when placed out of the English protection by the
act, which prohibited all commerce with them as
subjects, and permitted every species of hostility
to be exercised upon them as enemies, solemnly
declare themselves Independent States, by a vote
of Congress, dated July 4, 1776? Were all the
subsequent successes of the British arms, when
S   William Howe, with an armament capable of
       te   ith it into the most powerful
              had landed upon Long Island,
defea   all oppositio   , and seemed to be triumi-
phantly proceeding through the country, capable
of determining that body to rescind their vote?
Nay, when it was the opinion not only of the
majority of the English, but even of the greater
part of Europe, that they must fall a prey to the
immense exertions which were made against them,
did a single State swerve from the general confederacy, or abjure the independence which they
had declared?   If

If fuch was the inflexible refolution fhewn by the Congrefs and the American States, when the progrefs of the Britifh arms on every fide feemed to have prevented all future refiftance, and to have left them no other alternative, than death, or fervitude; when not an European nation had acknowledged their independence, or feemed inclined to fhare their dangers, by encou~~~~ the vengeance of their mighty foe; their ~~~~ tion and perfeverance have not appeared ~~~ ls uniform in that change of fortune which fucceeded.

In the Autumn of the year 1777, the brave and unfortunate General Burgoyne furrendered to the American militia at Saratoga, exhibiting a fatal example of the uncertainty of military glories, and the vanity of popular prejudices. About the fame time the decided intentions ~ the French to fupport the independc~~~~ ~f rica became apparent; and the ~~~~~ ~e the lofty pretenfions of the Britifh Miniftry to unconditional fubmiffion, produced the famous Conciliatory Bill, which paffed March the fecond, 1778. Thofe who remembered the frantic exultations of a confiderable party of this nation, at the fuccelfes which had attended Gen. Howe, in the Autumn of the year 1776, or confidered the filent contempt with which the American Petitions had been received at a ftill earlier period,

riod, could not but deplore the fallen ſtate of their country, which, in a ſpace of little more than two years, had exhibited every degree of inſolent deſpotiſm, and abjeƈt meanneſs. When the Americans had called upon the Britiſh nation by every tie of friendſhip, intereſt, and conſanguinity, to prevent the wild waſte of blood, and happineſs which was to enſue ; when they ſtated their complaints with moderation, or petitioned with temper for redreſs, it was deemed unworthy the dignity of the Britiſh Parliament to hear their reaſons, conſider their intreaties, or even to return an anſwer. The pretended repreſentatives of a nation, which dares to claim freedom as its right, publicly refuſed to three millions of men, the licence to ſtate their grievances, or implore redreſs ; and the profeſſors of a religion, promulgated by the loweſt orders of men, which breathes an univerſal ſpirit of peace and equality, and ordains, that he that is higheſt ſhall miniſter to his brethren even in the moſt ſervile offices of life, dared to treat their fellow-creatures, as if they neither owned a common nature, or creator, with themſelves. In the ſame ſpirit were the commiſſions framed which accompanied thoſe ſurer agents of peace, as it was then imagined, the military force. The commiſſions granted to General Howe, gave him no other power than that of

par-

pardoning all treafons and mifprifions of treafon, upon proper fubmiffion made to him by the Americans. This amazing condefcenfion towards men, who contended, that they were only fupporting their own juft rights, and who believed, that they had only taken up arms to avoid the laft conditions of fhame and fervitude, was attended with all the effect that its contrivers probably intended. Frefh indignation and hatred on the part of the Americans, who determined rather to perifh in one general wreck, than meanly folicit pardon, where they owned no fault, and had themfelves complained of injury. Yet notwithftanding thofe lofty vaunts and arrogance of the Britifh Miniltry and Parliament; notwithftanding the repeated victories which had attended our arms, and the utter ruin and defpair of the republican party in America, which was propagated and afferted in every corner of this ifland, we find the fecond fet of commiffioners, on the 9th of June, 1778, offering fuch terms to the rebellious colonies, as were not only infinitely beyond their own defires in 1775, but fuch as fcarcely left to this country the fhadow of authority over her revolted children. It may deferve the confideration of thofe gentlemen, who feem to imagine, that the Americans are to be drawn from their declared independence, from their folemn alliances, from their purpofes avowed to

Europe

Europe and all the world, by the firſt gracious overtures of a new Adminiſtration, to conſider what was the declaration of the American Con-greſs, dated April 22, 1778, upon the ſubjeƈt of this very commiſſion. They declare, " That any man, or body of men, who ſhould preſume to make any ſeparate or partial convention or agree-ment with Commiſſioners under the Crown of Great-Britain, ſhould be conſidered and treated as enemies to the United States. That the United States could not with propriety, hold any con-ference or treaty with any Commiſſioners on the part of Great-Britain, unleſs they ſhould, as a preliminary thereto, either withdraw their fleets and armies, or elſe, in poſitive and expreſs terms, acknowledge the independence of the ſaid States.", The anſwer of the Congreſs was exaƈtly con-formable to this declaration, and the whole ne-gociation ended in the continuance of the war, and the abandoning of Philadelphia, as a preli-minary to the total ſubjugation of America.

If ſuch has been the inflexible ſpirit of Ame-rica, during every period both of adverſe and proſperous fortune, I would wiſh to know upon what thoſe gentlemen found their opinions, who ſeem to imagine that the Americans will now treat with England, on terms ſhort of independence ? —Have our armies been attended with ſuch de-

D

ciſive

cifive fucceffes as may infpire this confidence? Have fo many nations acceded to our alliance, as may infpire them with doubt and terror? Is it the formidable ftate of our navy, our finances, or the internal proofs of virtue and confummate abilities which we have difplayed to Europe, that fupport this opinion? Or is it our brilliant fucceffes againft the *perfidious* Dutch, a new enemy flung into the preponderating fcale, and that mafter-piece of Britifh valour and policy, the capture of St. Euftatius?

I am the more interefted in bringing forward facts like thefe to the public attention, becaufe I have repeatedly feen the moment of peace and reconciliation flung away, by refufing thofe conceffions which would have purchafed them. Had we condefcended, in 1775, to confider the American petitions and grant redrefs; had we, in 1776, inftead of pardoning, in the true fpirit of a lawyer, treafon and mifprifion of treafon, offered them fecurity for the contefted points, there can be little doubt that the war would have been either prevented, or fpeedily concluded. Let the Britifh nation beware how, for the third time, they lofe the moment of fecurity which is placed within their power, light up the flame of civil war anew, and expofe themfelves to fuffer, in turn, the evils they have been fo long inflicting.

inflicting. Let them remember, that Carthage,
the great archetype of England, once covered
the feas with fleets, and aftonifhed the world
with the rapid augmentation of her opulence
and greatnefs; that fhe too aimed at diftant
conquefts and dominions, while Hannibal was
defolating the fruitful plains of Italy, and thun-
dering at the gates of Rome; but let them alfo
remember, that when the tide of fortune changed,
Hannibal was recalled for the defence of Africa,
and a fingle battle decided the fate of Carthage.

As to thofe who yet flatter themfelves that it
is in the power of this nation, either to grant or
to withhold the independence of America, I
muft intreat them to confider what it is which
conftitutes the independence of any country.
—Is it not the firm undeviating will of the
individuals who compofe it not to fubmit
to foreign domination, accompanied with the
actual exercife of fovereignty, and the power of
defending themfelves from all external violence? In all thefe refpects, is not America as
actually independent as any nation of Europe,
as independent as Great-Britain herfelf, would
fhe, for an inftant, lay afide her habitual arrogance, and confider her own internal fituation?
For upon what fhall we eftablifh our fuperior
claim? Is it upon a fhort continuance of inau-
fpicious peace, during which the nation has feen

almoft

almoft every poft of truft and power filled up
by men whom fhe hated or fufpected; the
facred rights of popular election invaded, the
ftreams of juftice itfelf fometimes tainted, fometimes reftrained; and every petition of the people treated with undifguifed contempt? Is it
upon a feven years civil war, into which the
moft refpectable, perhaps the major part of
this nation has been reluctantly dragged, and
forced to contribute to its continuance by expences almoft ruinous to the very exiftence of
their property, like malefactors that are con-
demned to carry the inftruments of their own
execution? Is it upon the patience with which
this people has borne the deftructive burthens
of the prefent war, the wild wafte of public
property, and the refufal of that moderate redrefs which Afiatic tyrants would fcarcely have
refufed to Afiatic flaves?——Or is it, laftly,
upon that vote of an uncorrupted Houfe
of Commons, which eftablifhes the exiftence
of public abufes, in thefe memorable words,
" that the influence of the Crown has been
increafed, is increafing, and ought to be dimi-
nifhed."

Should any honeft minds be offended at the
boldnefs which I ufe, I muft beg them to
confider that I do not mention a fingle circumftance, which has not repeatedly been afferted,

and

and reafoned from as fact, by moft of the
gentlemen who now compofe our Adminiftration; and I am not willing to lofe that happy
moment, which may, perhaps, never return,
when I find my own fentiments in perfect union
with thofe of the eftablifhed government. If
farther apology than this fhould be deemed neceffary, I muft reply, that we have been too
long intoxicated with the fumes of our ambition
and importance, too little interefted to confider our prefent fituation.—Too long a feries
of revolving years has feen us the flaves of
impofture and delufion, the prey of idle credulity, and the implicit victims of every interefted fiction. Every fpecies of parliamentary
and public information has been fo ftudioufly
withheld, that I much doubt if a fingle fact
has ever been offered to the people, fince the
commencement of the prefent war, upon which
we can entirely depend. In the mean time,
the good people of this country; that country
where the reft of Europe was accuftomed to
fend their philofophers, as ancient Greece to
Egypt, in order to ftudy morals and legiflation;
feems contented with the conviction of its own
eftablifhed greatnefs, to have confidered with
indifference every circumftance upon which
that greatnefs muft depend. Did a new dancer
arrive from the opera de Paris, who ftraddled
wider,

wider, or capered higher than his noble affo-
ciates, you might behold the genuine and undif-
fembled eagernefs with which the Britifh nobles
and fenators confidered the event. His agility,
his fhape, his antipoftures, his grimaces, nay, the
very ribbands which he wore, and the colour of
his breeches, were fcrutinized with all the anxiety
of intereft and inveftigation, during fucceffive
months. But did an immenfe continent revolt?
Was a naval battle loft, although its lofs might
fhake the very foundation of our naval and commercial greatnefs? Was a Britifh army captured,
or an ifland loft? It was juft whifpered upon the
Exchange, repeated at a city dinner, jefted upon
by a court Lord, and then configned to eternal
oblivion.

But it is now time for the Englifh nation to
roufe from that delirium in which it has dreamed
of conqueft and dominion, in the midft of
thofe luxuries and pleafures which not only inca-
pacitate it to command others, but even to preferve
its own liberty. If my countrymen wifely bound
their ambition with being the firft dancing and
fiddling nation in Europe, it is neceffary to refign
thofe fchemes of power and conqueft, which would
only ferve to draw their attention from thefe objects : but if fome remains of antient pride, and the
memory of paft glories, fhould rufh upon their
minds, and ftimulate them to new exertions, they
cannot

cannot too foon or too attentively confider their prefent fituation, left thofe exertions, like all the reft, fhould be ineffectual, and only exhauft the fafter their few remaining refources. Nations, like individuals, can only hope to fucceed while they proportion their enterprizes to their force, and wifely aim at poffibilities: that people will never be deferted by fortune, which is not wanting in itfelf, and which endeavours with fortitude and wifdom to atone for former rafhnefs. But violent and injudicious efforts, however they may flatter the public pride, will never alleviate the public diftreffes; they are lefs the fymptoms of health than the agitations of convulfion, which do not portend recovery, but approaching diffolution.

I cannot therefore too ftrongly inculcate upon my countrymen, the neceffity of mixing with that fortitude which is fo requifite in their prefent cir-cumftances, fome portion of that good fenfe for which they were once fo defervedly famous.— This, I cannot help believing, will evince, if pro-perly exerted, the neceffity of chufing one of the alternatives which I have mentioned; either that of profecuting the war againft the Americans, to fubdue them by force, or of granting their inde-pendence, and general terms of peace to all the nations we have irritated. Let the inhabitants of this metropolis, that fertile foil, where every feed of prejudice and abfurdity is generally found to

ger-

germinate with the rankeſt vegetation, recal for an inſtant, their own ſenſations in reſpect to the rioters of 1780. The outrages of thoſe unhappy men were partial, and affected but a ſmall number of individuals; yet let them recollect the general conſternation and horror which were produced in almoſt every mind; and which ſeemed, for ſome conſiderable time, to have extinguiſhed even national humanity. The ſtreets heaped with the dead and dying, during the military fury which raged for ſome days uncontrouled; and the yet more awful ſpectacles of promiſcuous and implacable juſtice, ſerved only to gratify the ſtern reſentment of the mildeſt people in Europe, and to fill them with ſilent ſatisfaction. The very eyes of the ſofter ſex, accuſtomed to weep for every trivial, for every fictitious woe, ſeemed to refuſe a tear for the numberleſs miſeries that ſurrounded them; ſo vaſt, ſo many are the ſacrifices which the jealouſy of invaded property demands for the ſlighteſt offence. This recollection, I ſhould think, might teach my countrymen to gueſs at ſome part of the ſenſations which muſt rankle in the boſoms of the Americans. They have ſeen their property laid waſte, their towns and cities conſumed, their country deſolated with all the fury that marks the laſt exceſſes of war, inflamed by civil hatred; every inſult has been offered to their women, every degree of ſcorn and inhumanity

nity to thofe who were taken prifoners, and every
fpecies of barbarity to thofe who refifted : even the
favage tribes, whofe manners are fometimes quoted
to exprefs a degree of atrocious cruelty beyond
the corruption of polifhed nations, were not judged
unworthy of the alliance of finging, fiddling,
Frenchified Britain, or agents improper to be em-
ployed in her domeftic quarrels: But it has pleafed
that Providence, to whom the folemn appeal of
both countries has long been made, to reprefs the
arrogance of this country, blaft her ambitious
defigns, and bid her vengeance and her infults
recoil upon her own devoted head; and now, difgraced and baffled with fmothered rage and una-
vailing pride, we reluctantly prepared for peace.
Are we yet to learn that the Americans are men ;
men that can feel as deeply as ourfelves the fenfe
of injury and injuftice; men that poffefs reafon
and paffions in common with ourfelves, and
haughty minds, ftimulated at once by vengeance
and elevated by fuccefs ?—If fo, what is there to
juftify the fond and foolifh prejudice which leads
us to imagine they will, at the firft invitation,
abandon in our favour all the alliances they have
contracted, entail perpetual infamy upon their
rifing name, and ftain with the imputation of
levity and falfehood, all the trophies they have
raifed ? Is it the old prejudice, that almoft a
fourth of the whole earth requires the affiftance of a

E   fmall

fmall damp ifland, placed at the diftance of many thoufand miles, in order to enable it to fubfift? Are we yet to learn that America poffeffes every variety of product which this country could ever boaft; all that the warmer funs of Spain and Italy can ripen, with thoufand others, denied to the induftry of Europe? Or do we believe that the choice and excellence of our manufactures will make them again accept our empire? This reafon, though better founded than the laft, will be found equally vain; for a more urgent neceffity preffes us to fell than them to buy, and every nation in Europe is preparing to extract her own advantage from our miftakes; every port is opening to their fhips, and every ftate foliciting their commercial alliance. Or perhaps it may be the bleffings of our envied and admired conftitution that may foften their ftubborn fouls; and they may pant for the fplendour of a civil lift, for the œconomy with which our finances are managed; for the bleffings of bifhops and hereditary nobles; for the intricate magnificence of our Gothic tenures; for a clergy to decimate their agriculture, without performing in perfon a fingle duty of their office; for a navigation act to improve their commerce; and for myfteries of a virtual reprefentation to fecure their freedom.

Let us for once be candid, and acknowledge that we have nothing, in our prefent fituation, to allure

allure the Americans to a participation; that men, who have toiled through feven bloody years to eftablifh their right to freedom will haidly throw away, without a motive, the harveft of their toils, and fubmit to wear the yoke which they had broken to pieces; let us allow that Providence, wherever it has given a fertile foil and temperate climate, has intended the human fpecies fhould exift and increafe, without afking the privilege from equals, who are feparate from them by the whole habitable earth, or half the extent of ocean; let us allow that men that poffefs reafon, induftry, and experience, and that have emancipated themfelves from the chains and prejudices of Europe, may provide for their own internal policy, and external defence, without the affiftance of Englifh lawyers or an Englifh Houfe of Commons.

Nor, could the fhadow of a connection, the chimera of a political union, be admitted by the keen-fighted, jealous Americans, can I conceive at prefent any other effects which would arife from it, but new wars, new mifchiefs, and new declarations of independence. Upon what terms, I afk, is it to exift? Is it to be a mere vague, unmeaning, undefinable acknowledgment of dependence, while their provincial governments retain all the attributes of perfect and unlimited fovereignty? Is fuch a paltry fubterfuge worthy to be

propofed

propofed by us, or granted by them? Would it not add ridicule to our difgrace, as if our pride was capable of being foothed with fo paltry a conceffion; as if we chofe to derive our titles from what we had loft, and like fome of our own noble fpendthrifts, to be only pointed out by the eftates we had alienated and fquandered? but we muft, I fear, pay an higher compliment to the great politicians amongft us, who are contending for fuch a fcheme.

They muft certainly have a wider reach, and intend to fecure fomething like a conftitutional fubordination in America, even though they give up the exploded principles of taxation, and permit the infringement of the Act of Navigation. But are we fo little acquainted with human nature, as not to fee that this would anfwer no other purpofe, than that of keeping alive a continual diftruft in the Americans, a continual jealoufy of intended encroachment, and would eternally prevent the ancient wounds from clofing? From the prefent Adminiftration I can, indeed, fear nothing, becaufe there is fcarcely a man amongft them, that is not perfonally pledged to the people for the integrity of his intentions, and for the redrefs of public grievances. But is their continuance eternal? have we not feen premature political death cut off as promifing adminiftrations, even in the bloom of fportive infancy?—Alas! who does

not

not know the thoufand unforefeen contingencies
that may deprive us of the fruits of their labours,
and change the prefent mild, pacific, unoffending
fpirit of our councils, into gall and rancour?—But
how is this fubordination to be fecured? Is it to
be guaranteed by Congrefs, or is it to be main-
tained by thofe *red-coated* citizens, who enforce the
execution of civil laws, under the denomination
of a military force? In the one cafe, I fear, left
the dependence fhould be merely nominal, although it produce moft of the inconveniences of
a real one; in the other, I dread, leaft the Americans fhould object to refigning every thing into
the hands of military guardians, without over-
awing them by a fuperior number of their own
militia. In that cafe, where will be their effi-
cacy?—Or were they nearly balanced, who
will infure the continuation of even a month's
agreement between high-minded men accuftomed to decide every thing by the fword, and
infpired with all the animofities which the prefent conteft has breathed into their fouls?
Should feuds arife, fhould blood be fhed, will
their refpective nations be unconcerned fpecta-
tors of the fray? And then the offices of ftate,
are they to be filled up by Congrefs, by the people of every ftate, or by the Britifh Minifter?
—Will the Americans acquiefce in fuch nomina-
tions? Will they fufpect no frauds, no influence,

no

no interference of the Treafury, no attempts upon their *Roman* virtue?—Or, fhould they fufpect fuch practices, however innocent, will haughty fouls like theirs tamely acquiefce, in fuffering Britifh gold to win its way where Britifh fteel has failed? Will they not return with tenfold fury to their beloved Independence, and will not every circumftance I have mentioned be fufficient to diffolve the feeble connection, or kindle the ill-extinguifhed flames anew?—

But I am reafoning about events, which are fo little likely to happen, that they fcarcely deferve a moment's confideration; and the two principal divifions of politicians in this country, cannot, without the laft inconfiftency, admit their probability for an inftant. Thofe who have always afferted, that the Americans have long defired independence, even prior to thefe unfortunate difputes, can hardly imagine that they will give up the darling object of their intrigues, the very fuft moment they have obtained it; and thofe who believe the affertions of the Americans themfelves, and the evidence of events, that every ftep they have taken in this affair, has been fuggefted and neceffitated by the perfecutions of this country, will not believe that they will, on a fudden, acquire fo much confidence in us, or retain as little in themfelves. It is now time for the Englifh to

lay

lay afide their foolifh contempt of men, who are defcended from their own nation, who boaft an equal fhare of all the qualities which have ever diftinguifhed it; and to believe that the Americans no more want ability in their councils, than valour in the field. Let us not then imagine them fo grofsly ignorant of their own fituation and of ours, as to grant to negociations what they have refufed to arms. Let us not imagine them either fo devoid of reafon, or of honour, or fo ignorant of their own effential interefts, as to enter into any treaty with us, which would cover them with the imputation of perfidy, and deprive them of the friendfhip and affiftance of the other nations of Europe. Were it even poffible that the great body of the people of America, for there is no virtual reprefentation there, fhould overlook the neceffary confequences of fuch a meafure, let us have a better opinion of the abilities and of the ambition of their leaders, than to imagine that they would fuffer them to accede to fuch propofals, without opening their eyes to all its poffible effects. We did not find them fo eafy to be deceived, or wrought upon, when the conciliatory propofitions of 1778 were fent over; and we muft have a very peculiar view of human nature, if we imagine that fuccefs is likely to render the mind more tractable and humble. Have we ever experienced thefe effects ourfelves ?

Let me now be permitted to enquire what are the advantages likely to enfue from a generous avowal of the independence of America. The firft advantage which I think will arife from it, is that of changing the entire nature of the conteft, and placing Great Britain in a lefs odious point of view to all the neighbouring nations.

When we take a retrofpective view of modern hiftory, we fhall find that almoft every people of Europe has, at fome period of their exiftence, been feized with the delirium of extending their power by conqueft; and of thefe bold difturbers of human peace, that there is fcarcely one that has not expiated its rafh exertions, by ages of inactivity and weaknefs. Venice, Portugal, and Sweden, have juft aftonifhed the world, like fhort-lived meteors, by their tranfitory greatnefs: Spain and France have fcattered terror and difmay, with the more continued blaze of comets; but both the former and the latter have refigned their place to England, who, unterrified by paft experience, rufhed forward in the fame mad career, and advanced rapidly to her decline. Europe, that had fo often feen her the patronefs of liberty, and the generous foe to tyrants, beheld her infatuation with mingled grief and pity, till, rouzed by the ftrong impulfe of intereft, or ir-

ritated

ritated by injuries, the different nations that compose it have either engaged in the conteſt, or prepared themſelves to repel the violence they dreaded, with equal violence. But this jealouſy of England, like the cauſes that have occaſioned it, is tranſitory and eaſy to be removed. The natural envy that att.. is a powerful and conquering nation, a want of moderation in the exerciſe of that ſuperiority, and the immenſe ſpoils which the emancipation of America from all commercial reſtraints promiſes to the different kingdoms of Europe, have been the cauſes that have indiſpoſed them againſt their ancient friend and ally. It may have been their intereſt, it may have been their paſſion, to clip the wings of her inordinate ambition, and to increaſe their own naval importance, by lowering hers. But the hour of Britiſh inſolence is paſt, the meaſure of her diſgrace is full, and it can neither be their intereſt or their paſſion that England ſhould be reduced beyond a certain point; ſtill leſs can it be their aim and objeæt to ſupport the maritime greatneſs of France and Spain, thoſe ancient and inveterate enemies to the common liberties of Europe.

Let England, therefore, give up the only objeæt which the reſt of Europe demands; an objeæt ſhe may yield with magnanimity, but cannot

F   withhold;

withhold; and from that inflant fhe will be en-
abled to make an honourable peace, or, if compelled to carry on the war, the principles and fortune of it will be changed. France has hitherto
had the addrefs to cover her ambitious views with
the fpecious femblance of moderation; fhe has
ccafed to be the common invader of all her neighbours, and the difturber of the general peace; fhe
is become the patronefs of univerfal liberty, the
guardian of public rights, and the difinterefted
championefs of the diftreffed. England, on the
contrary, from the unfortunate principles of the
war in which fhe is engaged, and from the head-
long fpirit of revenge with which fhe has profe-
cuted it, has loft the advantage of the ground,
and prefented herfelf to the eyes of Europe, too
much in the light of a proud, imperious conqueror. So long as fhe fuffers the contefl to be
carried on upon its prefent principles, that dif-
advantage will remain; and her crafty rival may
bereave her of all her moft valuable poffeffions,
with the appearance of defiring peace, and only
acting upon the defenfive. But let England once
defift from thofe ambitious fchemes of fubjugating
the Colonies, which have already coft her fo
much; and offering them the contefted points,
offer to her other enemies an equitable peace;
and France, who is the principal of her enemies,
will either be compelled to accept it, or to lofe
her

her prefent fituation. Not all the artifices fhe can then ufe, not all her policy, will then prevent her from appearing the aggreffor; and fhe will excite fo much the more jealoufy and fufpicion, as her prefent diffimulation is deeper, and her ambition more carefully concealed.

If we now confider the confederacy which is formed againft us, we fhall find it compofed of the moft difcordant and heterogeneous elements. All the States that conftitute it, vary as much in their refpective interefts, as they do in language, manners, prejudices and government. America with a wifh of which, perhaps fhe is fcarcely fenfible, to be reconciled to the parent ftate, provided England will treat her like a child that is arrived at maturity, and acknowledge her independence, is obliged to treat a nation, of whofe defigns fhe is fecretly fufpicious, with confidence and refpect. France, on the contrary, whofe darling object is to weaken the naval power of England, till it become inferior to her own, is fupporting a rifing empire, of which fhe either is, or fhortly will be jealous. Holland, irritated by the injuries and provocations fhe has received, by the invafion of her commerce, the capture of her fettlements, and the intrigues which fhe fufpects this country to have carried on againft her liberty, is waging a war of defence, of indignation, and of revenge. Spain, who had originally but little inducement to intermeddle, is

F 2

pro-

probably bribed with the hopes of recovering Ja-
maica and Gibraltar; and without farther confideration, intereſt, or paſſion, is combating to ag-
grandize an ally, againſt whom ſhe entertains a
fecret and hereditary hatred.—If the view, which
I have here prefented, of the intereſt and deſigns
of the feveral nations with whom we are involved
be juſt, it muſt appear probable, that the obſtina-
ty of England, in profecuting a war, to fubjugate
the colonies, and her impatience of every obſtacle,
have proved the ſtrongeſt bonds of confederacy
to her enemies. The æra, therefore, of her de-
fiſting from this deſtructive claim, whofe fatal confequences ſhe has fufficiently experienced, will be
the commencement of difcord and diſtruſt, amongſt
allies, whom accidental, not permanent intereſts
have united. France, herſelf, ſhould ſhe be guided
by enlightened and extenfive views of her own
intereſt, may be contented with the honour and
advantages ſhe has gained, and wifely fear a reverfe;
ſhe may perhaps perceive, that the project of de-
ſtroying the public credit, and exhauſting the refources of England, may, by a continuance of the
war, recoil upon her own head; and thefe con-
fiderations may make her as willing to accept, as
we are to offer terms of peace. As to Holland,
although the prefent impulfe of paſſion, and the
defire of revenge, may momentarily tranfport her
from her natural peaceable bias, there is little
doubt

doubt but fhe will be foftened, when fhe perceives a real and important change in the councils of this country; and that fhe will foon ficken of a war, where all the advantages will naturally center in her more powerful allies, and where victory, no lefs than defeat, may be prejudicial to her commercial interefts. As to Spain, as no particular interefts or paffions have led her into the war, fo we may not unnaturally imagine that fhe will be glad to free herfelf from the dangers and expences which attend it, by' feizing the firft opportunity of an honourable peace ; more efpecially if any unexpected misfortune fhould intervene, to abate the pride, which unwonted fucceffes may have raifed.

As to the other nations of Europe, I cannot retain a doubt, that they would then find it as politic to reduce the infolence of France, as they now have that of England, and that allies would not be wanting in fo juft a caufe, if neceffary. Nor would the advantage be lefs confpicuous, as to every purpofe of internal defence. For every difference of opinion muft then be filent, every murmur of difcontent and oppofition hufhed, when the immediate queftion related only to the common fafety of the country. What individual, that bore the name of Englifhman, would not feel himfelf rouzed to every noble exertion ? Who would refufe to contribute his property in any required portion, when he was certain it would be be applied to national defence, not to the wild purpofes of enflaving others, bribing the pretended reprefentatives of his country, or to fuſtain the luxury of proud unfeeling oppreſſors?—Who would even withhold his blood, if that blood was neceſſary to defend his own juſt rights, and fave his country's honor and independence from deſtruction? Thus, and thus only, would the refources of England be found really inexhauſtible; when every fcheme of felfiſh ambition was given up, when principles of juſtice were fubſtituted to the low intrigues and frauds that have long difgraced her councils, and when the Miniſters of the Sovereign, were at length become the friends and patrons of the public liberties.

A very confiderable portion of this nation has been long in avowed oppoſition to public meaſures; becauſe they believed thofe meaſures, with whatever fuccefs attended, adverfe to the intereſts and liberties of their country. Thefe men have been reviled with every odious epithet which ſlander, falfehood, and malice could invent: they have been reprefented as ferpents that were foſtered in their country's bofom, while they were watching every opportunity to ſting her to the heart. I believe that moſt of thefe gentlemen have treated fuch infinuations with the fame contempt that I have felt myfelf. But it is incumbent on all, that have avowed thefe principles of oppoſition, to

embrace

embrace the firſt opportunity of proving, that they are animated with as warm a zeal for their country's welfare, and dare as nobly in her juſt defence, as thoſe whoſe vaunts and menaces have been heard the loudeſt. It is alſo incumbent upon them to evince, that their attachment to America, has been the attachment of virtuous citizens, who think the real intereſt of their country can never be promoted by execrable and ſelfiſh ſchemes of enſlaving others; not a guilty preference of America to England. Nor can I doubt, though little inclined to pledge myſelf for the conduct of others, that ſhould the Americans once abandon the juſt grounds of ſelf-defence, and after having been of-fered the long conteſted independence, and terms of peace which they may accept conſiſtently with their treaties, league with the enemies of Britain for her farther humiliation, that from that inſtant, their warmeſt friends would become their moſt in-veterate enemies.

Something remains to be ſaid of the Americans themſelves; and as far as human reaſon may pre-tend to foreſee the future, theſe are the conſequen-ces which I ſhould think might be expected to ariſe from an acknowledgment of their indepen-dence. Perſecuted as they have been by the arms of Britain, ſtruggling at once for liberty and ex-iſtence, it is no wonder, if every former ſenti-ment has been ſuſpended, and if affection has

yielded

yielded its place to bitternefs and rancour. Still
lefs can we be furprized, if they fhould have found
a friend in every enemy to Britain, and have
gladly entered into every alliance that fupported
them againft her vindictive claims. Thofe, who
at the fame time that they juftified the Americans
in the firft periods of their refiftance to Britain,
have blamed them for their declaration of independence, and their treaties with France, feem to
poffefs but little acquaintance with human nature;
or even with the neceffary confequences of their
own principles. If fuch things exift as human
rights, which ought to be the bafis of every fociety,
and which, when once invaded, leave mankind
at large to confult their own prefervation, by fol-
lowing the dictates of reafon and experience; it
muft be granted, that the American independence
was not only juftifiable, but unavoidable. How
could men that had been deliberately placed out
of the protection of this country, and devoted to
deftruction, confider themfelves as owing any thing
to their deftroyer? Or how could that deftroyer
be confidered as the proper guardian of the very
rights which fhe had invaded, after they had been
fnatched from her oppreffion, by the bloody operations of the fword? Britain might, indeed, talk
of benefits, confanguinity, and gratitude, at the
very inftant that fhe was fpreading havock and de-
vaftation; and attempt to perfuade the Americans
that

that thefe were only fymptoms of her maternal care and her zeal for conftitutional liberty. But not all the fophiftry of her ablelt advocates, the diftinctions of her lawyers, or the pious hypocrify of her churchmen, can be expected to filence the feelings of our nature, or convert the exceffes of irritated pride into the effufions of tendernefs and affection. Thofe that believe tyranny to be the favourite attribute of Divinity, and that Providence had no other end in creating the innumerable millions which people the earth, than to foothe the pride, or employ the vacant moments of its lazy and befotted vicegerents, may be ftartled at every exertion of human liberty. But thofe, that in the human fpecies, behold an animal endowed, indeed, with nobler faculties, and deftined ultimately to an higher end, but agitated and impelled by the fame paffions which govern every other kind, will laugh at the opinion, that there are individuals only born for the fervice of others, or nations that are not to exift without the permiffion of their equals. When they are gravely told, that the Americans muft not make laws for their own government, becaufe they are originally defcended from the Englifh, they will afk, if the courfer that bounds along the mountains of Chili, muft not graze the herbage, or tafte the fpring, without the formal permiffion of his Andelufian brethren? Or whether the patient ox, that flowly breaks the

G   fallows

fallows of our weftern hills, may claim a right to difpofe of the immenfe Savannahs of America? They will afk, if there is any law of Heaven or Nature, more certain, more univerfal, more obligatory, than that of felf-prefervation; and whether Great Britain, when fhe obliged the Americans to draw the fword for their own defence, did not herfelf wave every other claim, and diffolve every other compact?——If, therefore, the Americans were right in the firft moments of their refiftance, it will follow, that they were right in every fubfequent one; fince the fame imminent neceffity continually impended; fince gratitude and perfecution, government and hoftility, are incompatible terms; and fince univerfal experience has demonftrated, that no human paffion is fo little to be trufted as difappointed ambition. That neceffity, therefore, which made them firft take up arms, produced their independence, and their alliance with France; and that independence muft incline them to league with every nation that is inimical to Britain, fo long as Britain retains the power and the inclination to annoy them. The bafis, therefore, of this alliance is mutual dread, and mutual jealoufy of this country; and the policy of thofe who think it is to be diffolved by a continuance of the war, unlefs we deem ourfelves equal to the conqueft of both nations, refembles the attempt of the North Wind in the Fable, to

make

make the Traveller lay afide his cloak; the keener blew the blaft, the clofer he wrapt his mantle round him, to defend him from its feverity.

But let Great Britain defift from her chimerical attempts to fubdue a country that is at this moment better prepared for internal defence than herfelf; let her either withdraw her garrifons from the American towns, or ftipulate to withdraw them upon fair and honourable terms; let her above all give every evidence, that under the propofals of reconciliation, fhe conceals no infidious project of renewing a war of conqueft, and it is probable that fhe may unbind the chain, which all her forces would never be fufficient to break. It is evident that from this moment the Americans will ceafe to confider the Englifh people as their foe ; that from this moment every former prejudice in their favour will be revived, and every antient affection recur to their minds. Their prohibitory laws will be repealed, their fhips, no longer fettered by the tyrannic influence of navigation laws, will voluntarily find their way to our ports, and their harbours in return will be open to our fleets. The induftry and ingenuity of our manufacturers will again find ample employment, when fo immenfe a market is opened to their exertions. In this fenfe, the colonies will ftill be ours ; ours in every rational and enlightened view of intereft, without infringing the rights of nature, or violating

the

the laws of humanity. Every increafe of population, or agriculture amongft them, will equally
contribute to our advantage, by the increafed demand for our commodities ; thus will they voluntarily alleviate our burthens, and bear without re-
pining, the enormous weight of the public impofitions here. And indeed, if we confider the
true interefts of this country, we fhall find that it
is commerce alone which had raifed us to our late
envied pitch of greatnefs ; and that it is by commerce only that we can hope to preferve fome
political importance, and the fhattered fragments
of our empire. We neither poffefs that vaft extent of country, or population, which can fit us
to afpire at dominion by conqueft. Above all,
our infular fituation, while it fecures us from the
fudden irruption of our neighbours, renders them
in turn more independent of us. For although
the empire of the fea, may in a certain degree
command refpect by land, yet I cannot recollect a
fingle inftance of any country's being conquered
by a naval invafion, that poffeffed even moderate
refources, or the common means of felf-defence.
The Carthagenians, who were deftroyed by Scipio,
in the third Punic War, conftitute no exception ;
fince they were firft exhaufted by their own im-
prudent efforts, and afterwards deferted by the
other nations of Africa, to whofe jealoufy the greater part of the Roman fuccefs was owing. Still

lefs,

lefs, can the conqueft of the new world by Cortez, in the fixteenth century, be admitted in oppofition to the rule; for there, the inequality of arms and difcipline operated with an almoft irrefiftible force; yet even that fuperiority would have been vain, had not the impolitic jealoufy of the Tlafcalans faved the common deftroyer from impending ruin, and firft eftablifhed the Spanifh tyranny in Mexico. But as Britain can never look for fimilar contingencies, fo fhe will be precluded from the dangerous delufion of attempting diftant conquefts, the inftant fhe properly confiders the nature of her own infular fituation. Happy indeed would it have been for her, had fhe perceived this great truth a little earlier. For had fhe caft even a fuperficial view upon fome of the moft important parts of her hiftory, fhe would have feen enough to ficken her with the very idea of carrying on an offenfive war, more efpecially at fuch a diftance, as muft inevitably render courage, policy, and even riches vain, if fhe had to do with enemies that were not wanting to themfelves. What end did all the decifive victories which fhe formerly gained over the French produce, but new toils, new contefts, frefh wafte of blood and treafure, and at length her final expulfion from every province which fhe had ever held? What were the effects in the beginning of the prefent century, of all the bloody wars about the Spanifh fucceffion?

fion? Did they not end, in fpite of all her boafted advantages, in the accumulation of her own debts, and the eftablifhment of the very competitor they were meant to exclude ? Have not the fame effects, at a later period, been the uniform confequences of every continental war fhe has waged. And in refpect to the prefent American conteft, did not every difpaffionate perfon foretell the event, or at leaft demonftrate, that whether baffled or victorious, fhe muft fuffer mighty loffes, fuch as fhe might never recover, without the leaft rational hope of advantage. For granting for an inftant, that the firft victories of the Britifh arms had been as decifive as they were fplendid, I cannot help deliberately afferting, that unlefs we had given up all the controverted points at once, and endeavoured to reconcile the irritated minds of the Americans, by reftoring to them all they had loft, the event might have been fomething later, but would have been precifely the fame as at prefent. As to the firft alternative, I leave good men to conjecture the nature of that conftitutional liberty which was intended for the conquered Americans; but I cannot help making fome reflections upon the fecond cafe, becaufe the ideas of conqueft, however fuppreffed by the little checks we have received in our career of victory, do not feem entirely extinguifhed in fome minds. Let us therefore fuppofe that the fame

expence

expence of blood and treasure, which at the end
of seven years has placed this country in a worse
situation, both as to conquest and defence, than
at the beginning, had produced a temporary cef-
sation of hostilities; and that after a certain number of civil and military executions, confiscations
of property, &c. &c. his Majesty's peace had been
successively proclaimed in all the thirteen provinces of America. May we not suppose, that the
same excellent policy which inclined our government to make war, in order to reduce the exube-
rant spirit of liberty in the colonies to the proper
bounds of loyalty and discretion, would have
judged it equally expedient to provide for futu-
rity, by modelling their respective governments
to that excellent system of constitutional liberty,
which is at this day found in Canada ? And would
not such alterations have probably left that leaven
of discontent, which would have made it necessary
to maintain a military force amongst the conquered,
amounting to at least forty or fifty thousand men,
to prevent future insurrections ? Must not that
military force have been continually increased
with the increasing population of America, which
is reckoned to double in about twenty years, to
prevent its becoming inadequate to its intended
object ? And would it have been an easy task to
govern eighty, an hundred and sixty thousand
men, and the indefinite multiples of that number,

ber, by orders from the War-Office here? Would
it have been agreeable to our gentlemen, who with
fo much true wifdom and found policy voted the
American war, in order to lower their own taxes,
to fee the land-tax doubled, trippled, &c. in order to pay their military deputies in America?
Or, can any one fuppofe, that the defolations of
fuch a war, as would have fubdued all oppofition
on that continent, would have left the inhabitants
any refources to pay fuch a peace-eftablifhment?
As there muft have arrived a term, beyond which
it was utterly impoffible to increafe the numbers
of our army there, would it not have been at
leaft neceffary either to prevent the farther increafe of population by an act of our omnipotent
Parliament; by deftroying a given proportion of
all the children that fhould be born; by felling
them as journeymen to the loyal manufacturers
of Liverpool, Manchefter, &c. or elfe to relin-
quifh at fome given period, the whole American
continent, and leave it to that independence which
we fo much dread? And laftly, would there not
have been fome danger in the mean time, that all
our ambitious neighbours in Europe, would have
continually caft an eye to America, as our moft
vulnerable part; and have required every real or
imaginary offence from us, by entering into
leagues with the exafperated colonies, fending
them effectual fuccours to excite new rebellions,

and

and lighting up new wars; till the utter ruin of this country had produced the final emancipation of all its dependencies?

It is not without particular defign, that I have entered into this digreffion; for I have feen my countrymen fo generally elated with the late trifling and accidental fucceffes, and forming to themfelves fuch mighty and chimerical expectations, which feem to embrace no lefs an object than the deftruction of the whole naval forces of all their enemies, that I cannot help trembling for the event. Convinced as I am, that there is no alternative between giving up the independence of America, and feizing the firft opportunity of making a general peace, or of engaging anew in all the horrors and difafters of a war of conqueft, which muft end in the utter ruin of this country, I cannot help attempting to rouze them from their temporary delirium, which is as little allied to real greatnefs as it is to found reafon and policy. For this reafon, I have ftated the confequences, which appear to me inevitable, had even the Britifh arms, in the commencement of the prefent war, been attended with the moft ample and unequivocal fuccefs.—But if we are to confider the fuccefs of Admiral Barrington, as the beginning of a new war, which fome of our politicians have afferted, let the Englifh people confider, while they are yet upon the fhore, the immenfity of that

H   fea

fea on which they are preparing to embark! What deluges of blood muſt flow, what millions of treaſure be conſumed, before this country could be brought back to a ſituation in which ſhe had the ſmalleſt hopes of ſucceſs! As to the united navies of our enemies, are they not confeſſedly to ours in the proportion of three to two ? Have not the French, in every engagement, given ſuch deciſive proofs, both of ſeamanſhip and courage, as to leave us no pretence to victory, upon equal terms, and frequently ſcarcely the poor conſolation of explaining away a defeat? Have not the Dutch, whom, in ſpite of Britiſh prejudices, I do not heſitate to name a brave and injured nation, given us ſuch unequivocal proofs of cool and inflexible bravery, that we ſeem ready to ſhrink from the conteſt which we had ſo wantonly provoked ? What elſe did all thoſe public rejoicings mean, upon the bare idea of a ſeparate peace with a people, whom, within ſcarcely the interval of a year, I have heard reviled with every odious epithet, in every part of this metropolis? I am too ſenſible, that truths like theſe, are little calculated to gain me either favour or popularity; and would ſome abler pen have undertaken the neceſſary and dangerous taſk of awakening the public to their own affairs, by telling bold unpalateable truths, I ſhould with pleaſure have continued in native unmoleſted obſcurity.—But ſince no abler advocate

has

has chofen to appear, and fince fome poffible good may arife from even thefe weak endeavours, if they fhould turn the public attention to the fober difcuffion of thefe important points, while all the rifk and danger are entirely my own, I fhall proceed with the fame fpirit 1 have begun, to the end of my fhort career. But if neither our former menaces to bereave the French and Spaniards of all their poffeffions in the Weft-Indies, nor our deeper laid defign, to crufh the Dutch at a fingle ftroke, have fucceeded to our wifh ; if every progreffive year has feen our loffes increafe, and our efforts diminifh in the fame proportion, how mighty, how complete muft be the madnefs that only propofes to end the war with the humiliation of all our enemies!—Are we yet ignorant that war, even in its moft fuccefsful ftate, is fcarcely lefs the fcourge of the victorious than of the vanquifhed party? Are we uninformed, that it is moft deftructive to a commercial country, that depends for its greatnefs upon a free exportation of its products and manufactures ? Do we confider the general failure of every branch of internal induftry, with the gradual aberration of the rich ftreams of external commerce, which formerly enriched us; thofe aberrations which it is yet uncertain, whether an age of peace and fecurity would completely bring back into their deferted former channels? Will

it

it not be neceffary, before we give a new fcope to
arrogance and enterprize, to reckon up the vaſt
arrears of the paſt, and to enquire whether the
probable fuccefles of a ten years war, againſt fuch
formidable opponents, will balance the certain
expences of a fingle year's delay of peace? Are
we not already burthened, beyond the poffibility
of farther endurance; burthened, till even the in-
ventive induſtry of miniſterial ingenuity is forced
to pauſe in its oppreffions; left, by the increafe
of weight unſkilfully applied, the overcharged
foundations ſhould give way, and the immenfe
fabric of debts and public credit fink, to rife no
more*? And is it in this fituation that the Engliſh nation employs itſelf in forming vifionary
fchemes of grandeur and command, which, were
they practicable, might afk at leaſt another feven
years bloody war, another hundred millions of
expence in the execution? In the mean time, the
numercus armies of America furround our few remaining towns, perhaps, fluſhed with the confidence
of victory, and puſhed on by the defire of vengeance, lead the fcanty remnants of our late victorious bands into captivity; perhaps, in the new
ardour of fuccefsful enterprize, roll back the tide
of war upon our late fecure poffeffions, and affiſt
our enemies to feize all that fortune has hitherto
permitted us to retain. At leaſt, even ſhould
theſe ideas be premature, the fatal progrefs of

our

our evil deftiny is continually accelerated, while we wafte the precious moments in empty dreams of chimerical exertions; the wounds which we have inflicted upon the Americans, are feftering with redoubled anguifh ; all Europe is preparing to acknowledge their independence, and folicit their alliance; the riches of their commerce, the only refource, I fear, which, even with an immediate peace, would enable us to bear an annual expence of fifteen millions,* are doled out to every competitor; and when fome new misfortune fhall rouze us from our trance, it may find us reduced fo low, as to wifh for a return of the prefent crifis, even at the expence of half our remaining territories.

Let us remember, that it is the characteriftic of light and frivolous minds alone to be elated beyond meafure with every tranfient ray of better fortune; to be eafily incited to form projects which exceed the compafs of their abilities, and to be always ready to throw the blame of paft mifcarriages upon every thing rather than their own rafh and chimerical projects. With fuch men, the change of a General, or of a Minifter, will at any time infure fuccefs, and encourage the moft extravagant expectations. They cannot believe that heaven, or fortune, will be fo unjuft

* See Lord Stair's pamphlet.

to their extraordinary merits, as to submit their
destiny to the influence of the common causes
which controul human affairs; or refuse to work
a miracle, whenever a miracle is necessary to extricate them from the effects of their imprudence,
Are they citizens, like the Romans, of a state which
has risen to importance by severer discipline and
stricter manners? They imagine that all the Gods
have fixed their residence in the eternal capitol, and
will continue to defend the chosen spot, although
every virtue which cemented its foundations is
withdrawn. But if their country, by a rare coinci-
dence of circumstances, an insular situation, a temperate climate, a system of laws which encourage
industry and secure private property, has arrived
at commercial and maritime greatness, they mistake these casual blessings for the inherent proper-
ties of their soil and climate. They imagine, that
they may with impunity engage in every vile and
pernicious project, and that their resources will
increase in the same proportion that they exhaust
and abuse them. Not even the rapid decline of
commerce, their own increasing poverty, the
miscarriage of their enterprize, the loss of their
fairest possessions, their acknowledged incapacity
to meet their enemies on the ocean, or their own
shores in consequence undefended, and exposed
to every invader, can make them abate their arrogance, or lower their pretensions: Nor should
I doubt

I doubt that fuch a people might gravely claim the empire of the fea, when it had neither commerce, fleet, or feamen left, provided fome happy genius fhould inftitute a naval proceffion, or, after the example of the Venetians, proclaim a marriage to be folemnized with the Atlantic.

But it is to be hoped, that the national good fenfe, when properly applied to the inveftigation of the fubject, will check the defire of military glory, and at length fettle in that only meafure which can produce any degree of public happinefs, a general and fubftantial peace. Peace is the firft and moft neceffary reform which is required. It is this alone that can reftore the almoft ruined ftate of our finances, if that reftoration be ftill poffible. A ftrict and uniform œconomy, applied with unremitting attention, during half a century of peace, might perhaps reduce the public debts within a moderate compafs: but what can be expected from our minifters during war, even though they poffeffed a degree of prudence and difinterestedness which have never yet appeared in man ? It is well known that all the fchemes of our greateft political œconomifts would never have made the public favings amount to half a million; while about three and twenty millions may be calculated to compofe the moderate purchafe of a fingle year's continuance of the war. Let my countrymen then ferioufly reflect upon the accumulation

of

of public debts, fuch as I believe was never experienced in any other country; upon the intolerable
burthens with which every article of convenience,
or neceffity, is already loaded; and upon forty
or fifty additional millions of outftanding debts,
which muft, in all probability, be directly funded,
and new taxes impofed to fupply the intereft, at
leaft if the declining commerce of the country can
fupport them, before new fchemes of enterprize
and conqueft are adopted. I fhould then wifh to
be refolved by fome of our ableft calculators,
whether the moft uninterrupted fucceffes would be
likely in any degree to pay the expences they had
coft; and whether the fee fimple of all the poffeffions we have left, excepting the monopoly of
the American commerce, which I cannot help
fuppofing out of the queftion, would indemnify
us for a two years continuance of the war. But
we have no reafon to expect fuch uninterrupted
fuccefs from any thing we have yet experienced;
and nothing but the moft childifh prefumption,
can found a fanguine expectation of better fortune, upon the mere remembrance of paft difaflers.
On the contrary, though we have been repeatedly
drawn in, like lofing gamellers, to hazard more
upon a frefh ftake, we have conftantly experienced
the fame cataftrophe; nor has there been a fingle
period of fix months, which has not degraded us
to a worfe fituation than we were in before, and
augmented

augmented our difficulties both, in refpect to making peace and carrying on the war.—But as to all the paft, however pernicious, however abfurd the conteft may have proved, however defervedly the authors of it may be reprobated as the deliberate enemies of their country, that conteft was lefs abfurd in the beginning, and lefs pernicious in the continuance than it would prove at prefent. It had then a precife and determinate object, however fatal both to humanity and public liberty, the exertion of the legiflative authority of Great Britain over the colonies, or, in more explicit terms, the eftablifhment of unlimited authority, and the reducing them to a ftate of unconditional fervitude. But this object, however execrable, was adapted to pleafe the vanity of a confiderable party in the nation, and few feemed able to difcern the immediate lofs, the ultimate fhame and ruin which might enfue. Although it required no great penetration to forefee that the attempts of this country to extend her authority by force over the colonies, might at fome future period produce their final emancipation, yet fuch was the apparent difproportion of the conteft, that even the cleareft underftandings might doubt concerning the immediate event. But with the prefent experience of our own weaknefs, and the force with which we are to engage, nothing fhort of madnefs can hope for fuccefs in a new attack upon the inde-

I

pendence of America. Indeed, the abfurdity would
not be more palpable, were we to revive our ancient pretenfions upon France, and fend over a
Mighty armament to annex the territories of his
Moft Chriftian Majefty to the crown of England.
Were we then to continue an offenfive war, it is
plain that it muft now be a war entirely without
an objeƈt, fince all hopes of fubduing the colonies
are at an end; and it muft be a ftruggle of mere
difappointed pride and refentment: paffions, which
cannot long influence the counfels of nations
without the greateft danger, even in their meridian
of power and fortune. But as to ourfelves we
have too long already been fubjeƈt to the influence
of thefe blind guides, and wafted too much in
rafh and vifionary purfuits. No farther projeƈts,
no farther experiments can be tried with fafety,
unlefs we choofe to deftroy our remnant of wealth
and power, as idly as we have diffipated all the
reft. That remnant, if wifely managed, is at leaft
fufficient for every purpofe of national happinefs,
though not calculated to fatisfy every demand of
national vanity. But whatever may be our wifhes
or expeƈtations, whether we are difpofed to con-
tent ourfelves with the folid enjoyments of fafety
and tranquility, or ftill afpire at dangerous pre-
eminence, peace is alike neceffary to the acquifition of either objeƈt. Peace alone can deliver
us from the enormous burthens with which induftry

duſtry is loaded; or at leaſt prevent the neceſſity of new oppreſſions; peace alone can revive our drooping commerce and agriculture, and enable us, by wiſe and ſalutary laws, and internal efforts at improvement, to increaſe our population and manufactures. Peace would enable us to turn our attention at leiſure, to the immenſe territories we poſſefs in India; a territory ſo vaſt, ſo fertile, ſo well peopled, that it might compenſate many of our loſſes, could we be convinced of the neceſſity of regulating it by wholeſome laws, adapted to the genius of the inhabitants, inſtead of making it the theatre where European plunderers contend for pillage. Peace would make us more reſpected in all the dependencies which we yet retain, and probably eradicate the ſeeds of future civil wars, if we do not think it below our dignity to be taught wiſdom by our paſt experience, or unworthy our greatneſs to redreſs the juſt complaints we have occaſioned by our former oppreſſions.

I ſhall now proceed to ſtate thoſe articles of the treaty of alliance between France and America, ſigned at Paris, February 6, 1778, which relate to the preſent ſubject, and prove the improbability of the colonies liſtening to any ſeparate terms of peace, before the acknowledgment of their independence. The ſecond article of that treaty expreſsly ſtates, that " The eſſential and direct end " of the preſent defenſive alliance is, to maintain

" effectually

" effectually the liberty, fovereignty and inde-
" pendence, abfolute and unlimited, of the faid
" United States, as well in matters of government
" as of commerce." The 8th article is " Neither
" of the two parties fhall conclude either truce or
" peace with Great Britain without the formal
" confent of the other firft obtained; and they
" mutually engage not to lay down their arms,
" until the independence of the United States,
" fhall have been formally or tacitly affured by
" the treaty or treaties that fhall terminate the
" war." This I fhould think is fufficient to prove
how vifionary and unfounded were the opinions
which lately prevailed with many of my countrymen, that the Americans would obey the firft invitation of this country to defert the French, and
even league with us againft them. Nothing but
the fame ignorance and inattention which have
guided every other part of our conduct could
poffibly have produced fuch a judgment.

But a more fpecious and important confequence
may be deduced from the articles I have quoted:
that even fhould the Englifh allow the independence of the Colonies in the moft unequivocal
manner, they are fo involved with France, that
they would not have it in their power to fufpend
hoftilities without the permiffion of their allies.
This interpretation is certainly not unauthorized,
and is a fufficient comment upon the wifdom of

thofe,

those, who, in spite of the most authentic information, suffered the Americans to enter into such
close connections with our enemies, at a time when
it is probable a little moderation and vigilance
on our part would have prevented them. But
when we confider the fense of the second article,
which explains and limits the nature of the alliance, we shall find that it exprefsly declares it to
be defensive for the purpose of maintaining the
sovereignty and independence of the United States.
Again, the 8th article confirms this interpretation
by limiting the duration of the war to the acknowledgment of the independence of America.
The obvious and literal fense of this treaty therefore is to ratify a defensive union between France
and America, for the purpose of establishing the
independence of the latter; and this end once obtained, leaves both the contracting parties at liberty. Nor can much doubt be entertained that the
Americans themselves will confider it in this light,
and not think it neceffary to carry on a war for
the interest of their allies, against a nation with
whom they have fo many natural connections;
and in whose favour we may rationally suppose
fo many ancient prejudices will arise, the inftant
all ideas of farther perfecution are removed. It
is the intereft of the contracting parties, which is
alone the guardian and interpreter of treaties between independent ftates; and this intereft will
evidently

evidently run as much in favour of England, when England difcovers unequivocal inclinations for peace, as it did before, againft her. It was. the intereft of France to feparate fo large a portion of territory from Great-Britain, whom fhe juftly confiders as her moft formidable enemy; it was equally her intereft to throw down all barriers to the American commerce, which opened fuch unbounded views to the ingenuity of her manu- facturers, and fuch ample refources to the em- barraffments of her finances. Nor was it lefs the intereft of the Americans to accept the overtures and alliance of every power which was hoftile to this country, and offered to fupport their inde- pendence againft its attacks. An alliance founded upon thefe principles, will neceffarily remain firm and indiffoluble, fo long as the common interefts of the contracting parties coalefce: but let either of them completely acquire the objects of its wifhes, and ample fcope is given to all the mo- tives of envy, jealoufy, and diftruft, to exert their power, and gradually corrode the bands of union.

Thus, it appears evident, in whatever light we confider the fubject, that acknowledging the in- dependence of America, is a neceffary preliminary of peace: for it will either fo completely fatisfy the intereft and ambition of all our enemies, that no material oppofition will be made to its ratifi- cation;

cation; or fhould it fail to have that effeɛt, will render the Americans fo luke-warm and indifferent to the common caufe, that we may naturally promife ourfelves happier fortune againft our remaining enemies.

Some gentlemen indeed feem to imagine, that it is not neceffary to make fuch facrifices, and that a reconciliation may be effeɛted with America, on terms fimilar to what we have granted the Irifh. But till they fhall take the trouble of explaining the reafons of this opinion, I cannot help thinking that it is more calculated to flatter the remains of national pride, than founded upon any real knowledge of the fubjeɛt.

It is no fecret that a commiffion has been fent over from the American congrefs to five commiffioners in Europe to treat of peace, whenever Great-Britain fhall be inclined to accede to thofe terms which are effential to its conclufion. It is alfo certain that feveral of the American agents, amongft whom Dr. Franklin may be numbered, have, both in their converfation and letters expreffed the moft fincere defire of terminating the prefent wafte of human blood, by a fpeedy reconciliation with this country; nor do I doubt that there is ftill fufficient affeɛtion remaining in the minds of many of the Americans, to make them defire every degree of profperity to this country, which is confiftent with the freedom,

interelt

intereſt, and honour of their own. It is alſo
equally certain, that not one of theſe commiſſioners, amongſt whom are included Dr. Franklin,
Mr. Adams, and Mr. Laurens, have ever given
the preſent miniſtry the leaſt hope that any part of
America would relinquiſh its independence, for
any terms or advantages propoſed by Great-Britain; on the contrary, I have every reaſon to
believe, that this has been the uniform language
of all the American agents who have been con-
ſulted upon the ſubject: " Great-Britain by her
" pride, her inſolence, her unjuſt attempts to re-
" duce the colonies to ſervitude, has compelled
" them to reſiſt by arms the intended invaſion of
" their rights. In the proſecution of this juſtifi-
" able reſiſtance, they have declared themſelves
" independent; becauſe, neither duty, compact,
" nor allegiance, can ſubſiſt between the oppreſ-
" for and the oppreſſed; between the nation that
" aims a mortal ſtroke at the exiſtence of ano-
" ther, and the people that takes up defenſive
" arms to vindicate itſelf from ſlavery and de-
" ſtruction. But Providence has uniformly blaſt-
" ed the ambitious deſigns of England, and fa-
" voured the ſtruggles of the Thirteen States, that
" through ſuch difficulties, through ſo many va-
" rious fortunes, through ſuch a ſtorm of blood
" and death, have perſevered in the generous
" deſign of maintaining the rights of nature and
the

" the common cause of the human species. If
" Great-Britain, unenlightened by all the past, un-
" taught by her own calamities, still persists in her
" former arrogance, and dreams of binding the
" hitherto unconquerable minds of the Americans,
" let her collect all her remaining forces, and ga-
" ther auxiliary troops of mercenaries from all
" the tyrants that deal in human blood, to make
" a last decisive trial of her fortune. She has
" already abridged all other rights, and severed
" every other tie, by appealing to the sword; and
" the sword is now the only charter of dominion,
" by which she must hope to rule over American
" subjects. Does she imagine that the ghastly
" wounds of a seven years civil war are to be
" closed in an instant by the charm of a fallacious
" lenity? Or that the Americans can so soon for-
" get the injuries they have received, their pro-
" perty wasted, their towns destroyed, their coun-
" try desolated, and every degree of hostile in-
" sult and cruelty offered to their families and
" themselves? Are these the potent arguments
" which are to induce them to resign the price
" of all their victories, and trust themselves again
" to the compassion of a British government, at
" the expence of all that is manly, just, or noble,
" either in nations or individuals? Is it for
" these benefits, so feelingly enforced, that they
" are to desert allies that have supported

K

" them in the hour of danger, cherifhed the rif-
" ing hopes of their infant ftates, and dared the
" vengeance and the fhock of the proudeft, if
" not the moft powerful nation in the univerfe ?
" Or does the fame delufion which made the En-
" glifh promife themfelves fo eafy a conqueft in
" the beginning, make them now imagine that
" the Americans are to be fubdued by policy,
" after having proved themfelves unconquerable
" by arms ? Why elfe do they think of propofing
" terms which they muft know would be rejected
" with fcorn by every people that is not delivered
" up to infatuation ? Shall the Americans brand
" themfelves with every epithet of perfidy and
" falfehood, violate the unblemifhed honour of
" their new republicks, and deprive themfelves of
" the future favour and affiftance of all Europe,
" that muft be witnefs of their fhameful ingrati-
" tude, only that they may deliver themfelves up
" to the very people that has been fo long armed
" for their deftruction.—They are not fo igno-
" rant of the feelings of eftablifhed governments
" towards thofe that are denominated rebels, or
" what they muft themfelves expect even from the
" moment of their accepting fo finifter a league.
" As to the pretended conceffions which are fome-
" times made to rebellious fubjects, they are at
" beft but authorized frauds, to difarm the intended
" victims of future cruelty and revenge. Is there
" in

" in all the wide extent of hiſtory, that baneful
" catalogue of human crimes and miſeries, a
" ſingle inſtance of theſe involuntary conceſſions
" which has not been revoked, without regard
" to faith or humanity, the very moment when it
" might be attempted with impunity ? And what
" is there in the nature of the Britiſh govern-
" ment, that ſhould produce an exception in its
" favour ? We are not ignorant of the mutability
" and inconfiſtency of its counſels; thoſe coun-
" ſels which ſometimes menace the ſecurity and
" independence of all the ſurrounding nations,
" ſometimes ſolicit peace with the holy fervour of
" primitive Chriſtianity. If the Engliſh themſelves
" repoſe an implicit faith in her new adminiſtra-
" tion, it is not ſo with the Americans, it is not
" ſo with the reſt of mankind. We know that
" the ſame breath which has blown up the bubble,
" that now dances upon the atmoſphere of nati-
" onal conceit, may diſſipate its unſubſtantial fa-
" bric, and breathe again thoſe peſtilential vapours
" which lately threatened the deſtruction of half
" mankind. As to the Engliſh themſelves, if they
" have voluntarily joined in this proſcription of
" the Americans, what faith, what confidence is
" to be given to a barbarous unfeeling nation,
" that only ſuſpends its cruelties from an inability
" to purſue them ?—If, on the contrary, as ſome
" pretend, they have been reluctantly compelled

to

" to fanctify outrages which they difapprove, on
" what pretence do they attempt to modify the
" rights of others, who are incapable of defending
" their own. Let them therefore underftand, that
" whether their characteriftic be cruelty or weaknefs,
" we will neither confide in the one, nor fhare in the
" mifchievous confequences of the other. We
" will remain fixed to that fpot where fortune and
" Providence have eftablifhed the foundations of
" our rifing empire, by the agency of our own
" fortitude and virtue. If England thinks that
" fhe can pufh us from the folid bafis on which
" we now ftand firm, let her approach with all
" her remaining forces, and make the dangerous
" experiment. If, on the contrary, fhe has had fuf-
" ficient experience of her own weaknefs, and wifhes
" to give the world and herfelf fome interval of
" repofe, let her, as a preliminary, defift from all
" the fchemes of wild and fruitlefs ambition. Let
" her equally lay afide the projects of fraud and
" violence ; nor attempt, by the contemptible
" arts of crooked policy, to deceive thofe whom
" fhe is unable to conquer. Let her meet the
" Americans with fincerity and magnanimity ; let
" her make all the atonement which is within
" her power to thofe fhe has injured, by defifting
" from new attempts to injure. As to our inde-
" pendence, in the ampleft fenfe that can be given
" to the term, we do not afk it of England or her

minifters

" miniſters, becauſe it is not theirs to give ; we
" already hold it from Heaven and the points of
" our ſwords ; and upon theſe alone ſhall we de-
" pend for its preſervation. Yet if ſhe fairly and
" honourably treat with us upon theſe terms, we
" ſhall acknowledge it as a proof of her ſincerity,
" and accept it as a pledge of offered peace. By
" theſe means, the memory of paſt injuries may
" be gradually obliterated, and ſhe may yet find
" in a participation of our commerce, the ſureſt
" prop of her declining opulence, and in our
" returning affection and future alliance, no con-
" temptible ſupport of her remaining empire.
" But let her at length underſtand the real limits
" of her power, and deſiſt from the attempt
" to unite and reconcile contradictions. The
" two alternatives are indeed before her,
" and ſhe may take her choice ; a firm and
" profitable peace, accompanied with the inde-
" pendence of the colonies, or a war of hatred,
" revenge, and fury to reduce the Americans to
" ſervitude, or periſh in the attempt. More than
" this, neither fortune, nor Heaven allows ; nor
" her own ungovernable madneſs, which has com-
" pelled the Americans to ſeize that independence
" which ſhe now in vain endeavours to withold,
" and compleated the diſmemberment of the em ·
" pire."

This,

This, or nearly this, I have reafon to believe, has been the language of the American agents, whenever they have been confulted: fhould I be miftaken, or endeavour to miflead, it will be no difficult matter to convict me of ignorance or falfehood. In the mean time, I cannot help fuppofing this reprefentation to be a juft one, and drawing fome conclufions from it, which merit all the attention of the public.

It muft appear evident, that no conclufion whatever can be admitted from the fituation of the Irifh to that of the Americans, excepting that a weak and oppreffive government will produce fimilar effects in every part of its dominions. The Irifh have obtained every thing they demanded: they afked for a free trade; that free trade has been granted them; they difclaimed the authority of the Britifh parliament; that point too has been given up; and they now declare themfelves, as they have every reafon to be, contented with the conceffions of the government. They have never voted themfelves independent, never entered into foreign alliances, never feen their country ravaged, or themfelves profcribed, under the pretence of reftoring conftitutional liberty and happinefs. There can be little doubt that the half of thefe conceffions offered to the Americans, when they petitioned in the year 1775, would have preferved their union with this country inviolate, and pre-

vented

vented all the mifchiefs which have fince enfued.
But that period is irretrievably paft, and never can
return. The colonies are now in actual poffeffion
of independence; they have conftituted internal
governments, which may perhaps leave them little
to regret in their lofs of the Britifh conftitution;
they have formed alliances with other nations,
upon the folemn compact of never again fubmit-
ting to a dependence, either upon this country or
crown; they have repeatedly foiled the attempts
of Great Britain to reduce them to her dependence, and refufed to treat upon any other foot-
ing than that of independent nations. What is
there in all this, fimilar to the prefent, or paft ftate
of Ireland; and what can be meant by the propofal of offering to the Americans the fame terms
we have granted to the Irifh, unlefs a pretext for
involving this country in all the miferies of a new
war, to fupport propofitions which we are fure
will be rejected with contempt?—Will thefe
terms be offered to the Congrefs?—But the Congrefs have no more power or right to accept them,
than the Britifh parliament would have to abdicate
the independence of this country, and make it an
appendage to France or Spain.—Nay lefs.—For
a Britifh parliament we all know is omnipotent;
an attribute which I believe has never yet been
claimed by Congrefs, who are only the deputies
of the feveral ftates, to tranfact whatever bufinefs

relates

relates to the common interests of the confederacy. Beside, we have some reason to guess at their sentiments upon this subject, by their treatment of the British Commissioners in the year 1778.— Shall we then offer these gracious terms to each of the several states that compose the American confederacy? But I have yet heard of no overtures from any of the provincial governments, which should make us hope that they would be accepted; and we know it to be a fundamental article of the American union, that any state, which shall presume to treat of a separate peace, shall be accounted a deserter of the common cause, and a public enemy. No way therefore would remain, as we can neither expect the Congress, or any of the provincial governments, to treat with us upon these terms, but to have the gracious proposals of a repentant government printed and dispersed over the country, for the benefit of individuals. And as the Americans have already had some experience of our methods of protecting them, I leave every one to conjecture the probable success of such a measure; more especially if we add to it the late vote of the House of Commons against carrying on an offensive war in America. In the mean time I should fear, that these inconveniences might result from such a step. The Congress would not fail to pass the most indignant votes upon the occasion; they, and all the friends of

the

the eftablifhed governments, would paint this conduct of the Englifh nation in the blackeft colours of perfidy and deceit. They would reprefent us as a nation devoid of honefty and fincerity; fo determinately inimical to the liberties of America, that we never, even when we affumed the moft pacific appearances, could lay afide the idea of enflaving the colonies; that, as our hoftilities were replete with every fpecies of cruelty, fo were our negociations with treachery and falfehood. What are thefe " pretended " offers, would they add, but a repetition of the " fame infidious arts, which they have fo often " ineffectually tried already? They know your " prudence, and your valour, when united; they " know that you are neither to be fubdued by " force, nor circumvented by negociation, and " therefore they again have recourfe to their " wonted arts, and attempt to diffolve that union " which renders you fo formidable. It is im- " poffible for that haughty nation to confider you " in any other light than that of flaves, eman- " cipated for a moment, but deftined fooner or " later to return to her domination. Even when " all the reft of Europe fhall have admitted your " independence, and folicited your alliance, you " will be honoured with no other title than that " of rebels by Great-Britain. The hatred that " fhe nourifhes againft you, for your emancipa-

L   " tion

" tion, is as unchangeable and eternal as her
" purpofe of reducing you again to her do-
" minion, and making you pay the accumulated
" punifhment of your too fuccefsful refiftance.
" This is the fpirit which alike animates her wars,
" and dictates her propofals of peace. In the
" one, fhe has ever been a cruel and vindictive
" enemy; in the other, fhe is a falfe, infidious
" friend. Even now, amidft all her profeffions
" of returning amity, fhe cannot hide the venom
" which is rankling in her heart, or conceal the
" intolerable arrogance which has fo long guided
" all her counfels.—Does fhe offer to treat about
" a peace fo neceffary to her own affairs?—It is
" in fuch a manner, as proves, that fhe ftill con-
" fiders herfelf as your rightful fovereign, and you
" as revolted fubjects, on whom fhe confers a
" favour, in remitting fome part of your merited
" punifhment. Though baffled fo often, and
" difgraced, fhe ftill treats with you as a fuperior;
" and thinks the honour of her alliance cheaply
" purchafed by you, at the expence of national
" honour and independence. Yes, that very in-
" dependence which you poffefs as abfolutely as
" any people in the univerfe, fhe pretends to mo-
" dify, and gracioufly contenting herfelf with
" bereaving you of more than half your rights,
" is willi g that you fhould hold the reft by the
" charter of her conceffion. But it is impoffible

that

" that you fhould be deceived by fuch contemp-
" tible arts as thefe ; or accept the olive as a pledge
" of peace, whofe leaves are incapable of con-
" cealing the ferpent which entwines its branches.
" Her offers are too openly infidious, and the
" malignity of her intentions breaks forth too
" glaringly, through the veil of diffembled friend-
" fhip, with which fhe endeavours to conceal it.
" She fees the impoffibility of conquering you in
" the field, and therefore has recourfe to nego-
" ciations, which fhe hopes may win their way
" where arms would fail. She wifhes to make
" you lofe the confidence of your allies, and the
" efteem of Europe ; thus will you be the more
" expofed to her future machinat She
" wifhes to fcatter feuds, difunion and inftruft
" amongft the feveral ftates that compofe the
" American confederacy, and to arm them cne
" againft the other, that the whole may be more
" eafily oppreffed and enflaved. This is the
" reafon why fhe refufes to treat with thofe
" whom you have appointed to be the arbiters of
" peace and war. She knows too well their vigi-
" lance, their prudence, their inflexibility ; fhe
" fears to meet the guardians of your liberty in
" council, as much as to encounter your armies
" in the field ; fhe therefore endeavours to enfnare
" the ignorance and credulity of individuals, and
" by fcattering fecret difcontents and jealoufies,

L 2   " to

" to open a way for her ufurpations. But go-
" vernments that are founded upon principles of
" juftice, and who claim no power but what is
" given them by common fuffrage, are unac-
" quainted with the fears and low fufpicions which
" never fail to accompany tyranny. We there-
" fore fubmit her propofals to you, confcious
" that there is but one light in which every friend
" to American liberty can confider them. Nor
" do we fear, that thofe who have toiled fo
" nobly through fuch a conteft, to eftablifh the
" foundations of the only free governments in the
" univerfe, will tamely yield, without an equiva-
" lent, the reward of all their labours."

Should any one be difpofed to treat me as the
advocate of American independence for expa-
tiating upon thefe topics; without either confeffing
or denying the charge, I muft obferve, that it is
entirely foreign to the purpofe. No one can
doubt that the Congrefs will refufe our overtures
for the future dependence of America, fhould fuch
overtures be made. Nor will they be contented
with a fimple refufal; it is equally certain, that
they will employ their whole addrefs to reprefent
thefe overtures, in the blackeft colours, to the
body of the people. Whether they are actuated
by a noble ambition of raifing the glory of their
country, or by the low defire of preferving their
own authority alone, this will equally be their
conduct.

conduct. Even the advocates for propofing to the Americans terms fimilar to thofe we have granted the Irifh, are of this opinion; fince they affert, that neither the agents of the French, nor of the Congrefs, will be able to prevent the reconciliation which they imagine muft be the confequence of fuch liberal conceffions. No one therefore can accufe me of fingularity for entertaining an opinion, which is even admitted by thofe who differ widely from me as to the reft; and the reflections which I have attributed to the Congrefs, are fuch as muft prefent themfelves even to the moft fuperficial underftandings.

Placed as I am, at an awful diftance from the profound myfteries of government, I cannot pretend to decypher accurately the intentions of our rulers. Many circumftances may make it inexpedient that the mazes of ftate-policy fhould be expofed to vulgar eyes; and therefore we ought to wait with a becoming patience, for the fuccefs of thofe negociations which are now carrying on. But it is impoffible for any man who has been an anxious witnefs of the public calamities, during the prefent ill-omened conteft, not to form conjectures about the future. Thefe conjectures it is the diftinguifhed privilege of every Englifhman to dare to offer to the public; the meaneft citizen enjoys this right in common with the proudeft; and the experience of fome paft years does not

tend

tend to prove, that either virtue or ability is engroffed by thofe who poffefs the higheft ftations.

I fhall therefore obferve, that the terms now offered to the Americans, either contain an acknowledgment of their independence, or propofals for fome limited dependence on this country. In the firft cafe, there is little reafon to doubt, that they will be attended with the defired fuccefs : and a peace will be no longer delayed than till the different claims of the contending parties can be adjufted. On the fecond fuppofition, I will venture to predict, that all propofals for the dependence of America on Great-Britain, however modified, will be rejected with fcorn by the Congrefs, and all the ruling powers in that country. I have fufficiently ftated my reafons for this affertion; but it is a fpeculation of the moft interefting nature to enquire, what will be the conduct of our minifters in cafe of fuch a refufal.

Some perfons may poffefs that fervour of imagination, which may lead them to think, that the revolution of power in this country will produce a fimilar one on the other fide of the Atlantic. They doubtlefs dream, that when the Britifh offers fhall be difperfed over the country, the people will either compel their rulers to accept them, or take up arms to depofe both Magiftrates and Congrefs; that all America will forget both republicanifm and independence, and unite to celebrate the praifes

praifes of a patriot adminiftration, in a tranfport
of gratitude and loyalty. As to myfelf, whatever joy it would give me to fee the inhabitants of
Bofton and Philadelphia approaching the throne
with loyal and conflitutional addreffes, I cannot
help fearing, that we are far removed from fuch an
aufpicious æra. We know that the attachment
of mankind, either to national manners or forms
of government, bears no proportion to the comparative excellence of the objects; if indeed it be
poffible to eftablifh a criterion to judge of things
which are reducible to no common principles, and
which vary with every guft of national prejudice
or opinion. All the reprefentations of European
elegance or enjoyment, would no more tempt a
Kamtfchatkan from his cave, or an Iroquois from
his foreft, than the love of favage liberty and independence would induce an Englifh nobleman to
throw afide the trappings of his exalted flation,
and take refuge in eternal fnows, or pathlefs de-
ferts. How often do we fee the opinions that in
one country are treated as the excefs of wicked-
nefs and impiety, confecrated by altars, priefts,
and temples, amidft their neighbours; while the
reverence for a particular name or family, which
is confidered as loyalty and honour on one fide of
a river or mountain, fhall be reprobated as treafon
and rebellion on the other!—Whatever reverence,

therefore,

therefore, we may feel for the Englifh conflitution, whatever bleffings we may imagine it capable of imparting, it is impoffible to deny, that the Americans may entertain very different ideas upon the fubject. The fplendour of a court, the advantages of an hereditary monarchy, the facred name of King itfelf may be in fome minds fo ftrongly affociated with the ideas of unlimited power, and the purpofe of enflaving mankind, that they may excite no favourable impreffions. Whether from reafon, obflinacy, or error, we know that thefe are the fentiments of the Americans; at leaft a large, if not the largeft part of this nation has been accuftomed to reprefent them in this light. But if the natural bent of their difpofitions has long inclined them to independence and republicanifm, it will be difficult to affign a reafon why they fhould entertain more moderate ideas at prefent.

But fhould they perfift in thefe ideas, fhould they reject the offered terms with the contempt which I am perfuaded they will feel for every propofal of dependence, what conduct is this country to obferve?—Are we to depart, at length, from all our lofty pretenfions, and grant the long-contefted boon; are all the fine-fpun fchemes of political connection to be diffolved; all hopes of returning allegiance to be facrificed; are fifty thoufand lives, and an hundred millions

of

of treafure to be wafted in vain, and only to cement the foundation of thirteen republican ftates: or will our minifters, animated by a noble defpair, pafs all the bounds which they had before prefcribed, and heedlefs alike of their own profeffions and the infamy which muft attend fuch grofs inconfiftency, openly engage themfelves in a new war to fubdue the Colonies?

This enquiry is of fo much importance, that the illuftrious characters who compofe the prefent adminiftration will certainly give the people complete fatisfaction upon the fubject. They know how much we have already fuffered, how repeatedly the public confidence has been abufed already by former minifters; they have long and feelingly arraigned the bafe duplicity and falfehood which ufed to prevail in our councils; and it is to refcue us from evils like thefe, not from avarice or ambition, or the felfifh defire of advancing themfelves upon the ruin of others that they have accepted the reins of government; every motive of honour, fhame, confiftency muft incline them to a nobler conduct; nor will they deceive our wifhes, or adopt the execrable arts to which we owe fo many miferies.

Should they therefore be convinced that the dignity of the crown, the fpirit of the conftitution, the unity of the empire, require new wars, new facrifices, and the impofition of heavier burthens,

M they

they will at leaſt treat the public with ſincerity, and acquaint it with the important change in their ſentiments. This change may indeed happen, becauſe there is the greateſt difference between a miniſtry and an oppoſition, and many ſources of information and motives of conduct muſt occur to the one which are totally denied the other. But they will lay before us the reaſons which they now find to expect ſucceſs, in ſchemes which they have ſo often declared impracticable; they will ſtate the remaining reſources of the nation that inſpire them with theſe hopes, the intended expence and probable duration of the war. They will not inveigle us from year to year with falſe eſtimates and fallacious hopes; nor will they delude the unwary innocence of the country gentlemen with promiſes of lowering their taxes from the confiſcations and forfeitures of America. Should it be neceſſary to ſend over new armies with better auſpices, they will not do it under the mean pretence of defending ports, or garriſoning towns. They will alſo, I hope, think it neceſſary to aſſign the limits of their own exertions, and the period at which we may expect ſome reſpite, whatever be the fortunes of the war. Wherever theſe limits may be fixed, whether at public bankruptcy, a ſeizure of all private property for the uſe of government, or the general depopulation of the land, it will be ſome alleviation of our diſtreſſes, to look forward to a certain termination; and it will enable thoſe who want faith or loyalty to wait the laft extremity, to feek over the habitable globe fome afylum from the bleffings of the Englifh conftitution.

In the mean time I fhall endeavour to ftate thofe reafons which induce me to believe that our prefent adminiftration have either already acceded to the independence of America, or mean to do it, if that condition fhould be infifted upon as a preliminary of peace. Thofe gentlemen while they were out of power have been accuftomed to make the American war the fubject of their fevereft and moft popular invectives. According to them, the defign to fubdue the colonies was equally unjuft, abfurd, 'and ruinous. All the forces of the Britifh empire were inadequate to fuch an attempt, and public bankruptcy muft be the neceffary confequence of perfifting in the enterprize. With what energy, with what eloquence have they defcanted upon our declining commerce, our involved finances, the diftreffes of our country gentlemen, the miferies of the poor, and all the complicated calamities which this unnatural quarrel has produced. How often and how feelingly have they adjured the late adminiftration to ftop the ravages of war, to reftore peace to an exhaufted nation, and to offer the Americans fuch terms as they were likely to accept. With thefe fentiments fo often, and fo folemnly expreffed, they have entered upon the management of public

M 2

affairs,

affairs, in order to rescue their country from its difficulties by a speedy peace. But it is impossible they could mistake the terms upon which alone it was attainable. They were not ignorant of the treaties the Americans had entered into with France, of the answers of the Congress to former propositions, of the representations of the American agents; every thing concurred to enforce the necessity of independence, as a preliminary or condition of peace. Unless therefore they intended giving up this article, their invectives and their professions must have been alike empty and insincere. For what was the crime of the last administration, at least after the commencement of the war, and the treaty of alliance, but refusing to grant the independence of America, and prosecuting the war to make her forego that claim? That administration never refused to treat on terms short of independence, nor did the Americans ever make any conciliatory proposals to that purpose since the year 1776. But those ministers had repeatedly declared, that they never would acknowledge the independence of America, or desist from war till the colonies had given up the claim; and it was to save us from the inevitable ruin which must have attended so rash and absurd a resolution. that the rising spirit of the nation has produced the present happy change. But this change has not been effected merely that

the

the people might be amufed with a vain fhadow of negociation; this was a tafk for which our late minifters were as well qualified as their fucceffors. Nor was it from the hope that the Americans would recede from their haughty declarations of independence, in favour of a new adminiftration; fuch a fyftem might amufe the politicians of a coffee-houfe, or the editor of a newfpaper, but was too ridiculous and unfounded to be adopted by men of fenfe, who poffeffed the genuine fources of information. Leaft of all was it, merely that the conduct of the war might be fhuffled from one hand to another: it is the war itfelf, and not the management of it, that the late oppofition have fo fuccefsfully arraigned; nor have they ever fucceeded fo well in proving the incapacity of the late minifters for carrying it on, as in demonftrating that the propofed end itfelf was chimerical, unjuft, and unattainable. But it was to ftop the ravages of that pernicious war; to vindicate our declining commerce and agriculture from new and more intolerable burthens; to reftore plenty to their country, and peace to Europe, that men of milder principles, the patrons of public liberty, and the genuine friends of the people, have been elevated to the honours they now enjoy.

Hence it feems to follow, that every friend of the prefent adminiftration fhould ftrenuoufly vindicate them from the fufpicion of meditating any

coerciv

coercive war againſt America. Such a charge
muſt either include the excefs of folly or duplicity—folly, if they alone were ignorant of faĉts
which every man of common abilities or information clearly underſtood; and duplicity, if all
their declamations in favour of peace meaned nothing more than to acquire the management of the
war. But that degree of ignorance was abſolutely
impoſſible: nothing therefore remains but to ac-
cuſe them of the groſſeſt inſincerity. For if, in
the preſent ſituation of England, the public intereſt required that we ſhould carry on a war to reduce our colonies to ſome modified degree of
dependence, what muſt we think of men who
have uniformly oppoſed the very meaſures they
are compelled to adopt at laſt? We know too
well the uncertain nature of war; that an opportunity once loſt is frequently never to be regained;
and the influence which the opinion of vigour and
perſeverance exerciſes over the minds of men, ſo
great and univerſal, that mankind are much oftner
conquered by their own fears than by the prowefs
of their enemies. The laſt miniſtry had ſome
title to both theſe qualities; they laviſhed the blood
and treaſures of the nation as profuſely as if cen-
turies of duration were compriſed in the preſent
moment, and as if America once nominally ſub-
dued would ſet us free from any future ſtruggle;
nor did they ever pretend to humanity or remorſe;
they

they plainly declared, with a moſt laudable ſincerity, that if they could not conquer America,
they wiſhed to render it an uninhabited deſert, a
ſmoaking pile of ruins. This was plain and manly; it was alſo conſiſtent with a certain ſet of principles, which has generally had the ſanction of
divines, and, for the curſe of human nature, has
always been the favourite creed of princes and
ſtateſmen. But what would have been the conduct of their antagoniſts upon the ſuppoſition I
am now examining? Equally convinced of the
fatal neceſſity of theſe meaſures, they muſt have
uſed their whole addreſs and influence to render
them abortive, when their ſucceſs would have
been attended with leſs loſs and blood-ſhed than it
would be at preſent; or elſe, againſt their own
conviction, they muſt become the miniſters of
cruelty and injuſtice, and deſolate the world merely that they may preſerve their places. The ce-
lebrated vote of the Houſe of Commons againſt
proſecuting an offenſive war with America, was
certainly the work of the late minority; and this
vote was a plain confeſſion to all the world of our
weakneſs and inability to purſue the war. That
vote, with more than magic force, arreſted all
our military operations, diſarmed our veteran
bands, and added confidence and intrepidity to
their enemies. That vote was a compleat abdi-
cation of all our boaſted ſovereignty over America,
and

and gave additional stability both to the Provincial governments and the authority of the Congress.
For is it possible that after such a declaration we
could invite a single American to join our banners,
or expose ourselves to his derision, by promising
our protection ? To me indeed, and to every man
that is not possessed with the chimerical rage of
making conquests, that vote appeared the only
mark of public sanity which we have shewn for
many years. Considered as the pledge and har-
binger of approaching peace, it seemed wisely calculated to abate the animosity of the colonies, and
merited all our gratitude and approbation ; but if
it was nothing more than a public leger-de-main
to juggle the cards out of hand into another, it
certainly was the grossest instance of public ab-
surdity that ever was exhibited. Nor would it
solve the objection to suppose, that no offensive
war was to be waged with the Americans, but
only with the French, till they gave up the treaty
of alliance and the independence of the colonies.
If the French demand immoderate terms of peace,
we shall be compelled to carry on a war, not
against the independence of America, but for our
defence. But it will be necessary to prove this in
a satisfactory manner, both to this nation and to
Europe at large, by exposing the terms that had
been offered by us, and refused by them, other-
wise it must appear the vilest political quibble that

ever

ever difgraced a nation; and only intended to lull one enemy afleep, till we had difpatched the reft, and could return with additional force for his deftruction. Such conduct I am afraid, inftead of ferving, would only prejudice our caufe in the eyes of all mankind, by adding the imputation of treachery to hat of violence ; and would fo totally alienate the Americans, by raifing unconquerable fufpicions of our fincerity, as would render all reconciliation impoffible.

Nothing therefore remains but to fuppofe, that as our minifters are men of fenfe, and pledged to the people by every motive that can act on generous minds, they really mean to purfue that conduct which honour and public utility equally require; and to give us that peace, which it is certainly in their power to beftow, and which our difficulties and diftreffes fo loudly demand. This is certainly the wifh of the founder, and I believe at prefent of the moft numerous part of the nation; and the experience of every hour will add new converts to the opinion. Whatever may be the frantic exultations or chimerical projects of a few, the wifer individuals of every party, think that we have made a fufficient trial of fortune, and that the prefent ftrength of our enemies is fo over-proportioned to our own, that it is a fufficient glory to have been fo well able to act upon the defenfive. They fee that the project of deftroy-

N   ing

ing the navies of France, Spain and Holland, is as
chimerical as it is unjuſt; and that were it more
practicable than it is, the reſt of Europe is too intent upon its own commercial intereſts, to ſuffer
the balance of naval power to be entirely deſtroy-
ed. and ſo great an acceſſion of ſtrength thrown
into hands that have not always uſed it with the
greateſt moderation. As to America, all parties
are now agreed, excepting a few hot-headed zea-
lots, that ſhe has nothing to fear from the attacks
of England; and that no future connection can
ſubſiſt between the two countries, but the volun-
tary ties of friendſhip and mutual intereſt.

In this ſituation, ever thing concurs to make
the people deſirous of accepting peace, and to induce the miniſtry to grant it. Every order of
men will rejoice to ſee a termination of public
difficulties and impoſitions, excepting the few who
might have promoted a vile, partial intereſt, by
the continuation of the war. Whatever may be
the murmurs of that ſet of men, they will ſoon
ſubſide, extinguiſhed by the voice of a grateful
nation, that will ſooner or later learn, by its own
comparative feelings, the difference between a full
and ſafe enjoyment of the fruits of its induſtry, a
circumſtance ſo neceſſary to all, and the empty
triumphs of ſuch a war as we now carry on always balanced by contrary fortune, and attended
by increaſing poverty and diſtreſs. Theſe reflexions

flexions appear to me fo folid and unanfwerable, and at the fame time fo important to this country in the prefent moment, that I could not refift the impulfe of laying them before the public; whatever perfonal danger or inconvenience may attend the publication of unpalatable truths, fo little difguifed by artifice or flattery, that they may difguft even thofe who cannot difpute their authority.

It may be afked, why I alone have thus flood forth, and pretended to inftruct a nation. Many will tax me with folly and prefumption; many will arraign me as the friend of America, and enemy to the glory of my country; fome may perhaps accufe me of fecret intereft, or difguifed ambition. As to any of thefe charges, I fhould confider them with indifference and contempt, did not the nature of my fubject itfelf prevent me from paffing them over in filence. I fhall therefore obferve, that what I have here advanced, is little calculated to gain me either patronage or popularity; none but the real, difinterefted friends of their country, will either excufe the doctrines, or the boldnefs with which they are enforced; and the only character I can ever expect to gain by means like thefe, is, that of a turbulent, difcontented man, incapable of leaguing with any party, and dangerous to all. As to the prefumption which I have ufed, it is no greater than

becomes

becomes a man, than, I think, becomes an Englifhman; every one is equally interefted in the welfare of that fociety of which he is a member; the
meaneft can but lofe his all in common with the
greateft; nor are the trappings of ftate and gew-
gaws of a crown of more importance to the
monarch, than his cottage and humble fare to a
peafant: neither nature, reafon, or juftice, has
given to a few individuals the right of judging for
all the reft.

But as to the heavier charge of favouring the
liberties of America, far from attempting an apology, I fhall both confefs and glory in the accu-
fation. England is indeed my country; there was
a time when I gloried in the name; and I will
prefume to fay, that few have fhewn themfelves
more completely Englifh, either in their principles
or conduct, than myfelf. But I have never been
able to cherifh an exclufive partiality for any
country at the expence of juftice and humanity;
and were I capable of doing it, the refult of all
my experience tends to convince me, that the
real intereft of no fociety ever was, or will be
promoted by fyftems which contradict the plaineft
principles of morality. The wideft range of
empire, the moft uninterrupted fucceffes which
have attended the guilty projects of ambition,
have never produced any other effect, than that
of

of hurrying nations fo much the more rapidly to their decline.

And much would it conduce both to the fecurity and happinefs of mankind, were this great truth more clearly underftood, or more univerfally adopted as the principle of action. We might then expect to fee honeft ends purfued by honourable means; and a care of the effential interefts of the people fubftituted to the paltry intrigues and machinations which have fo long been the difgrace of courts and ftatefmen. Thofe who claimed fuperior privileges, or engroffed the powers and diftinctions of fociety, would think it neceffary to deferve them by other arts than a contemptible luxury, an habitual practice of low diffimulation, or a blind acquiefcence in thofe pernicious fchemes which alike fap the foundations of liberty and public happinefs. In peace, we fhould fee them intent on repairing the ravages of war, improving every means of national defence, regulating the morals, and adding to the convenience of the people. Their care and wifdom would correct every abufe, before it increafed to a dangerous magnitude; nor would the art of legiflation remain the greateft reproach to the human underftanding, and the leaft improved by the progrefs of reafon and philofophy. The laws, whofe clearnefs and intelligibility are fo effential to the happinefs of the people, would be adapted to

common

common ufe and underftandings; not by reducing
them to one general principle of promifcuous def-
potifm, an improvement which many of their
profeffors are fo defirous of introducing, but by
difentangling them from the cuftoms and per-
plexity of barbarous ages, from the doubtful force
of contrary decifions, and all the unmeaning rub-
bifh in which they are now involved. Commerce
and agriculture would flourifh, not by the regu-
lations of boards of trade, or the thoufand abfurd
and contradictory provifions which difgrace our
ftatutes, and deter the honeft mechanic from the
exertion of his ingenuity, but by fecuring to every
man the produce of his labours, freeing induftry
from unneceffary reftraints, and bounding the
incroachments of that all-devouring monfter the
excife. Were it neceffary to engage in wars, thofe
wars would be fo clearly juft and unavoidable,
that there could be no difpute about the expedience
of fupporting them: a wife œconomy would
manage thofe refources which are drawn from the
labours of the people, nor would the public confidence itfelf be made a reafon for its abufe, or the
public patience an apology for the profufion of a
government.

Thefe indeed are vifionary fchemes, fufficient
to interrupt the gravity of a minifter, fhould he
condefcend to read them, or move the rifibility of a
financeer. The deeper projects of modern policy

are

are of a very different nature : they confift in melting down the vigour of a nation by private and public corruption, tolerating every fpecies of abufe, invading the people's property by intolerable taxes, and under that pretence fubjecting the moft innocent and indifferent actions to reftraint. Wars of the moft deftructive nature are entered upon for every purpofe but that of national utility ; and peace itfelf brings no alleviation of public burthens, nor always prevents their accumulation. At length, unnerved and harraffed, entangled on every fide with the inextricable well of debts, taxes, and penal laws, as well as infected with the fecret venom of all-pervading influence, a brave and generous people refign all claim to privileges it has long difufed, forgets that ever it was free, and finks into the eternal fleep of fervitude.

And fo univerfal have been thefe arts, fo general their fuccefs, that when we contemplate the different regions of the globe, we fhall find they have almoft all in turn become the victims of avarice and ambition. Afia has been the feat of immemorial tyranny ; Africa fees all its coafts depopulated to fatisfy the demand of Chriftian luxury for flaves ; Europe itfelf is on the point of yielding to the common deftiny. Government, that partial benefit, but univerfal evil, becomes, even from the moment of its inftitution, the engine by

which

which the interests of the many are submitted to the caprices of the few. But moderate at first in its pretensions, and fearful of exciting too powerful an odium, it veils its baneful innovations under the semblance of order, public safety, and national defence. At length, like a stream, which flowing through an immense extent, has been gradually swelled into a torrent, by the recession of a thousand rivulets, it rises over every barrier, and deluges all, with irresistible fury. Mankind have then no other choice, but to worship the idols of their own creation, or to be exterminated by the sword which they have foolishly trusted to other hands. From that instant, there are no bounds to insolence on one side, or degradation on the other. The noblest empires seem only created for the sport and riot of a few conceited families; all the productions of the earth are monopolized; the elements themselves become subject to human pride; and man that believes himself the lord of all, is the only animal that starves amidst universal plenty.

This is the progress of every government; and however retarded in its course, it as invariably tends to despotism as rivers seek the sea by the laws of gravitation. Can any generous or humane mind, therefore, that is convinced of this truth, behold with disapprobation the struggles which are made in any corner of the globe for liberty.

liberty. Will he not wifh to fee the fpoilers of the world, the enemies of common happinefs, checked in their courfe, and new afylums opened to the fuffering part of the fpecies? But fhould the conteft happen in the very country of which he is a member, will not a much more powerful motive intervene, his own immediate intereft; at leaft if he has learned to attach other ideas to the term than that of perfonal eafe or fafety, or the wifh to fhare the plunder, and riot in the fpoils of others?

It is upon thefe motives that I confefs I have uniformly detefted the American war. No example could arife from the fubjugation of that country, excepting a repetition of the common cruelties, which under the name of juftice or policy are practifed in all conquered countries; and particularly in thofe where public violence is ftimulated and excufed by civil animofity. The leaft that could have been expected, would have been executions, banifhment, confifcations of property, and the eftablifhment of a military government to extinguifh every fpark of liberty before it fhould begin to flame. I cannot pretend to affign the limits of minifterial mercy, but thofe that begin by invading every acknowledged right, and demolifhing every public barrier, will rarely end by replacing them. On the contrary, the fuccefs of the United States affords an awful fpectacle, which

O   cannot

cannot be too often renewed for the inftruction of mankind, and the information of fovereigns. It teaches the poffeffors of power, to ufe that power with moderation, unlefs they would incur the hazard of lofing what is fo dear to their ambition. It teaches mankind at large, that neither the vaunted prowefs of mercenary armies, the poffeffion of unequalled riches, fleets that command the ocean, or all the refources of eftablifhed authority, are fufficient to prevail over minds that have once determined to meet death rather than fubmit to flavery. Above all, the eftablifhment of fo many free ftates upon the pureft principles of civil and religious liberty, affords the moft confolatory profpects to every friend of humanity. The fame fpirit which has directed their foundations may ftill extend their limits, till the immenfe continent of America become the feat of happinefs and population, and the refuge of all the miferable, from European tyranny. How different is this view of things from that which the narrow f. e s of felfifh policy would have prefented! The policy which rather than emancipate mankind wifhed to wage war with Providence, and ftop the courfe of nature; to defolate the nobleft portion of the univerfe, and rather make it the receptacle of noxious reptiles and beafts of prey, than fuffer it to be inhabited by men that dare to

think

think for themfelves, and defend the privileges of
their exiftence.

Thefe were the general principles upon which
I always reprobated the American war; but when
I confidered its probable confequences upon the
fafety and happinefs of this country, motives of
private intereft concurred to augment my juft abhorrence. It was too evidently begun upon principles which had no connection with public
utility, however the public credulity might be
enfnared to fuffer its continuance. The intereft
of every people confifts in a due adminiftration of
the laws which defend their perfons and their
property, in a plenty of thofe things which the
fuftenance of life requires, and in a freedom from
thofe reftraints and impofitions which have fo
baneful an effect on commerce and agriculture in
other parts of the world. Could any thinking
man believe, that thefe falutary ends would be
promoted by the defolation of America and the
deftruction of its inhabitants ?—Thofe gentlemen
and merchants who affented to the meafure, with
the laudable intention of lowering their taxes, and
encreafing their markets, muft explain their own
ideas : to me it always appeared evident, that war
could neither promote our commerce, nor diminifh
our burthens. Could the burning of towns, and
the deftroying every fpecies of property, increafe
the American demand for Britifh commodities, or

contribute

contribute to the employment of our manufacturers? As much as the extinction of liberty
in America, and the establishment of a military
government there, would have tended to preserve
our rights at home, and diffuse the blessings of the
English constitution.

But every thing that the oppofers of that dif-
astrous war predicted at its commencement, has
since been fatally accomplished. Our burthens,
instead of being diminished, are increased to that
enormous magnitude which threatens the annihila-
tion of commerce and agriculture. The neighbouring nations of Europe, instead of viewing
with indifference or applaufe the chastisement of
our rebellious colonies, have ranged themselves
on their fide, as was foretold; and whatever may
have been the original strength of the Americans,
they have been fo well fupported by our ancient
enemies and rivals, as to baffle all our past, and
to be fecure from all our future attempts. Instead
of that contribution, which was the avowed object of the war, we have loft the monopoly of
their commerce, and must become, if we wish to
regain any part of it, fuppliants to thofe whom
we difdained to acknowledge as our equals. More
than an hundred millions have been already fquandered without the reduction of a single province;
and more taxes impofed on national induftry
than I will venture to fay, the exertion of mini-
sterial

fterial œconomy will deliver us from in the en-
fuing century; though it fhould uniformly proceed in the fame rapid torrent with which it has
begun.

In the midft of thefe diftreffes, a gleam of hope
breaks forth, if we deign to profit by our paft
mifcarriages, and to learn wifdom from misfortune. Our late fucceffes will facilitate the means
of peace, if we are ferioufly inclined to propofe or
accept the terms which are adapted to our fituation. Our enemies wearied with the ravages and
loffes of a doubtful war, will eafily confent to
breathe from their toils ; the Americans will gladly return to their former peaceable occupations ;
and all Europe will lofe its jealoufy of a nation,
that even in the midft of victory can refign the
fpirit of conqueft.

But perhaps the meafure of our calamities is
not yet full, and the pride and folly which have
fo long oppofed our happinefs, may demand fe-
verer expiations than any we have yet offered.
Our late fucceffes, indecifive as they are, and inadequate to any other objects than the acquifition of
peace, may raife new dreams of conqueft, and re-
new the general infatuation. A people long accuftomed to be deceived, too proud to yield, too
indolent to reflect, too corrupted to be juft or humane, may infift on kindling again the flames of
war, and deluging the earth with blood. A minifter

nifter felfifh and interefted like his predeceffors, may feel more attachment to pomp and power than to the effential interefts of his country ; with boundlefs ambition, but a contracted heart, he may take advantage of popular delufions to violate his own profeffions; or yielding to that mighty influence againft which he has fo long declaimed, may fteer the public veffel towards the very fhoals he has fo repeatedly pointed out, and inftead of making the port, feek for refuge amidft the ftorm.

In this cafe, I cannot expect to avoid the general fate, or to efcape that ruin againft which I have in vain endeavoured to warn my country. But amidft all the calamities which I forefee will burft upon us, it will be fome confolation to me, to have difcharged the duties of a virtuous citizen ; and without intereft or ambition, without even the wifh or hope of fame, to have oppofed myfelf to the ftream of public prejudice, and enforced thofe falutary truths, upon which depend the fafety and happinefs of the people.

F I N I S.

6. GENERAL CONWAY's MOTION for PEACE with AMERICA. In Red and Black Characters. Price 2d or 12s. per Hund.—A Correct and Complete LIST of the GLORIOUS MAJORITY on the Right Hon. GENERAL CONWAY's Motion for an Addrefs to his Majefty, for the Purpofe of procuring a Reconciliation with America, on Wednefday, February 27 ; as alfo Lifts of the Minority and Abfentees on that Occafion. To which are added, A few fhort Remarks on the Conduct, Converfation, and Connections, of feveral Members who voted with the Minifter on that Evening, by Way of Supplement to the Red Book, by the Help and Comparifon of which, it is humbly prefumed, a pretty fair Account may be collected for fo large a Minority on fo popular a Queftion.

7. A LETTER from Mr. DAWES to JOHN HORNE TOOKE, Efq. occafioned by a Part of his Speech to the MIDDLESEX FREEHOLDERS, at HACKNEY, on the 29th of May, 1782. Price 1s.